the
Wisdom
of the *Vedas*

the Wisdom of the Vedas

(Originally published under the
title *India's Outlook on Life*)

Jagadish Chandra Chatterji

L. |

*This publication made possible with
the assistance of the Kern Foundation*

The Theosophical Publishing House
Wheaton, Ill. U.S.A.
Madras, India/London, England

© 1973, The Theosophical Publishing House
All rights reserved.

First Quest edition 1980. No part of this book may be
reproduced in any manner without written permission except
for quotations embodied in critical articles or reviews. For
additional information write to: The Theosophical Publishing
House, 306 West Geneva, Road, Wheaton, Illinois 60187.
Published by the Theosophical Publishing House, a
department of the Theosophical Society in America.

Library of Congress   in Publication Data

Chatterji, Jagadish Chandra
  The wisdom of the Vedas.
    Published in 1931 under the title: India's outlook on life.
        1. Vedas. 2. Philosophy, Hindu. I. Title,
        BL1115.C45   1973   294'.1   80-51550
        ISBN 0-8356-0538-8 (pbk.)

Printed in the United States of America

PUBLISHER'S NOTE

All who seek understanding of the basic philosophies of the East will find in this book an illuminating presentation of the great Vedic system of thought, India's oldest and most profound religio-philosophical tradition. The author is Indian, with an unusual ability to frame the subtleties of Eastern thought in a manner easily grasped by the Western mind. "It may safely be said," comments Prof. John Dewey in his Introduction, "that nowhere will the reader and student find available such a comprehensive and clear account set forth by a competent authority."

The book was originally published in 1931 as *India's Outlook on Life,* with "The Wisdom of the Vedas" as a subtitle. It is being issued in this edition with these titles reversed, as more truly representative of the magnificent concepts set forth. A few minor editorial changes have been made, and the more unfamiliar diacritical markings on Sanskrit words have been eliminated, as they are likely to prove distracting to the general reader for whom the book is intended and to whom they have no special significance.

As the book is dedicated "To the friends of India in America," this edition is offered as a contribution to that great bridge of friendship between East and West which can come only from deeper mutual understanding of the two approaches of life.

We sit as in a boundless Phantasmagoria and Dream-grotto; boundless, for the faintest star, the remotest century, lies not even nearer the verge thereof: sounds and many-coloured visions flit around our sense; but Him, the Unslumbering, whose work both Dream and Dreamer are, we see not; except in rare half-waking moments, suspect not. . . . Then, in that strange Dream, how we clutch at shadows as if they were substances; and sleep deepest while fancying ourselves most awake! . . . This Dreaming, this Somnambulism is what we on earth call Life; wherein the most indeed undoubtingly wander. . . .

Nevertheless, has not a deeper meditation taught certain of every climate and age, that the WHERE and WHEN, so mysteriously inseparable from all our thoughts, are but superficial terrestrial adhesions to thought; that the Seer may discern them where they mount up out of the celestial EVERYWHERE and FOREVER: have not all nations conceived their God as Omnipresent and Eternal; as existing in a universal HERE, and everlasting Now? Think well, thou too wilt find that Space is but a mode of our human Sense, so likewise Time; there *is* no Space and no Time: WE are—we know not what;—light-sparkles floating in the aether of Deity!

So that this so solid-seeming World, after all, were but an air-image, our ME the only reality: and Nature, with its thousandfold production and destruction, but the reflex of our own inward Force, the "phantasy of our Dream."

—THOMAS CARLYLE, *Sartor Resartus,*
BOOK I, CHAPTER VIII

CONTENTS

The Supreme Critic on the errors of the past and the present, and the only prophet of that which must be, is that great nature in which we rest as the earth lies in the soft arms of the atmosphere; that Unity, that Over-Soul, within which every man's particular being is contained and made one with all other; that common heart of which all sincere conversation is the worship, to which all right action is submission; that overpowering reality which confutes our tricks and talents, and constrains every one to pass for what he is, and to speak from his character and not from his tongue, and which evermore tends to pass into our thought and hand and become wisdom and virtue and power and beauty. We live in succession, in division, in parts, in particles. Meantime within man is the soul of the whole; the wise silence; the universal beauty, to which every part and particle is equally related; the eternal ONE. And this deep power in which we exist and whose beatitude is all accessible to us, is not only self-sufficing and perfect in every hour, but the act of seeing and the thing seen, the seer and the spectacle, the subject and the object, are one.

—RALPH WALDO EMERSON, *The Over-Soul*

Preface

The present exposition of India's Outlook on Life, which is based ultimately on the Veda, has been prepared in response to repeated requests for a concise and comprehensive statement as to how the Veda, the most ancient wisdom of India, regards life, its origin, purpose, and goal. The writer knows of no other publication which covers this entire ground in so short a compass. It is believed, therefore, that the following presentation of the subject will prove serviceable not only as an introduction to a deeper and wider study, but also as a convenient summary of the salient points.

Ancient as it is, this view of life, when properly understood in all of its implications, may very well throw a flood of light on many an unsolved problem—philosophic, ethical, religious, social, and even scientific—of these our modern times.

Professor E. Washburn Hopkins and Professor S. Radhakrishnan have kindly glanced through these pages in proof and sent the author appreciative comments.

It is a great pleasure to acknowledge with gratitude the courtesy and kindness of Professor Dewey, of Columbia University, who, despite the pressure of multifarious duties, not only found time to examine the work with care, but also very graciously consented to write the Introduction to this little volume.

JAGADISH CHANDRA CHATTERJI

NEW YORK
JANUARY 14, 1931

Introduction

It would be difficult to find one less fitted by previous study and knowledge to write an introduction to an account of Vedic philosophy than the present writer. But, with the increasing intellectual contact of the East and West, it is obviously of importance that we of the Western world should have authentic information regarding the culture of India. The philosophy associated with Brahmanism is an essential part of that culture. In some respects knowledge of it is a key to the historic thought of India. Not only all scholars, therefore, but all interested in promoting spiritual exchange between the East and the West will welcome the series of publications of which this is the initial number.

Even one who, like myself, is not expert in Vedic philosophy will recognize the system, thoroughness, and lucidity with which Pandit Chatterji has presented that philosophy. It may safely be said that nowhere will the reader and student find available such a comprehensive and clear account set forth by a competent authority. It is not necessary to say to the Western reader that the foundations and the method of this Oriental system of thought are far removed from those current with us; it is not easy to translate from one system into the other. This very fact increases the value of the complete and clear statement which is set before us. It gives a much needed chart of bearings.

JOHN DEWEY

COLUMBIA UNIVERSITY
MAY 5, 1930

11

THE WISDOM OF THE VEDAS

PART I

The name Veda (or, as in the plural, Vedas) literally means Wisdom or Science, but is given, technically, to the oldest literature of the Indian people. This literature, going back to thousands of years before the beginning of the Christian era, consists traditionally of two definite groups, known as Mantras, which are the primary compositions, and Brāhmanas, which are a sort of illustrative commentary on the Mantras. In the following pages, too, the name will be used in the same traditional sense, meaning the whole collection of both the Mantras and the Brāhmanas, and therefore including, of course, the famous ten or twelve Upanishads.

Neither in the Mantra nor in the Brāhmana portion are the Vedas a systematic treatise on the Vedic view of life that is to be presented here. Yet all the elements of this view are to be found scattered in the different parts of the Vedic literature and have been gathered together and treated systematically by various writers from very early times.[1] What is to follow here is a similar, though very brief, treatment of the Vedic material on the subject. This treatment follows, moreover, the general traditional under-

[1] Cf. R. D. Ranade, *A constructive survey of Upanishadic philosophy* (Poona, 1926), esp. chap. 4, "Roots of later philosophies." See also Deussen, *The Philosophy of the Upanishads* (Edinburgh, 1906) and the first volume of his *Allgemeine Geschichte der Philosophie* (2d ed., Leipzig, 1907), dealing with the philosophy of the Mantra part of the Vedas; S. Radhakrishnan, *Philosophy of the Upanishads* (London, 1924).

standing of the matter, but in a manner which is intended to facilitate its comprehension by those not specially acquainted with the ancient Aryan way of viewing life. The Vedic view of life, then, both as reflected in the literature of the Vedas and as followed in India to this day, may be summarized as follows:

There is nothing absolutely stable, nothing permanently abiding, in the whole of the objective universe, which is but a system of ceaseless "goings on" (*jagatī*, collective movement) with everything in it continually moving and changing (*jagat*).

This ceaseless movement in the universe, however, is not merely a mad dance; there is method in it and the movements are arranged in groups and "made to dwell" (*āvāsya*) within limits and for periods of various lengths, so as to give them what looks like stability, more or less enduring.[2]

What gives the systems of movements this apparent stability, orderly arrangement, and regulated sequence is not any property of the movements themselves, but is something other than the movements, being a power that rules them (*īsh*) and "makes them dwell diversely" and in order.

The exact nature of this power, whether feeling or unfeeling, conscious or unconscious, intelligent or unintelligent, whether absolutely stable and abiding or only apparently so—all this cannot possibly be definitely known nor can the power be directly contacted by way of the movements. Indeed, the movements themselves are cognized not directly but only inferentially as the cause of the sensations which alone are experienced directly and intimately. The power ruling the movements is thus doubly and impenetrably veiled from us by the sensations direct-

---

[2] *Īshāvāsyam idam sarvam yat kim ca jagatyām jagat* (White Yajur-Veda 40.1 — *Īshā Upanishad* 1).

ly experienced and by the movements inferred as the sources of the sensations.

But while our entrance to the core of things by way of the senses is thus effectually barred, there is nevertheless a gateway of direct approach to what lies beyond the veil of sense perceptions and even beyond the movements, and, standing there, imparts that apparent stability and order which we experience in regard to the ever-fleeting show of the objective universe. This gateway of entering directly the heart of things is, however, one which can be discovered only if we turn our attention away from the objective universe and dive down deep into what constitutes the subjective nature of every one of us as an individual. "Nowhere else is there a way of reaching" the heart of the universe.[3]

It is true that, in regard to what we are as individuals subjectively, equally as in the objective sphere, all is movement. We find that our bodies as well as our thoughts, feelings, ideas, and all mental states, i.e all that conglomerate vaguely called the mind or soul—all these are continually moving and changing; in all of them there is nothing whatsoever that is absolutely stable and permanent.

Still we have a feeling—an illusory feeling, no doubt—that even though we, as individuals, be only ever-shifting aggregates of "mental states" and "complexes" and equally ever-changing aggregates of bodily cells, we are yet somehow stable and abiding entities, so that every one of us has the experience: "I am one and the same person yesterday, today, and the day after—the same John Smith from childhood to death." And illusory as is the feeling of stability and continuity in regard to the ever-changing complex of an individual ego or soul, this illusion, like all others, must have a basis in fact and in an actual

---

[3] Cf. *nā' nyah panthā vidyate 'yanāya,* Shvet. Up. 6.15.

experience of the fact. This fact is to be found in
the presence—as the ground of our existence, and
back of all mental states and all physical aggregates,
and, as it were, wrapped up in them as in so many
coatings (*kosha*)—of an entity that does not change,
and is, therefore, a timeless Being (*sat*). And we
have the direct experience, however vague, of this
Being in the uttermost depths of our existence: we
feel that we *are*. In the Vedic language, this Being,
in the aspect that constitutes the ultimate Self and
ground of our existence, is called Ātman; but in
translating Ātman, as used in this connection, by
"Self" one has to bear clearly in mind that "Self"
here is not anything like what is generally understood by the English words "mind," "mental states,"
or even "soul" and individual "spirit." The "Self,"
as an equivalent of the ultimate Ātman in man, is
other than all mental states, other than even "spiritual" states, such as feelings of love, joy, charity, and
the like, insofar as these also come and go, grow and
decay, and are subject to change. The Ātman is
what substantiates these mental and spiritual states,
so that they are then felt and experienced as the
individual ego or "I."

As the Ātman or ultimate Self in the individual,
this ever-abiding, timeless Being is "smaller than the
small" (*anor anīyān*), that is, infinitely small, and
has no measurable magnitude. Anything that has a
magnitude which can be measured, no matter how
small the magnitude—anything, in other words, which
is not either infinitely small or infinitely great—is
perishable, is not abiding. There is no example
anywhere in the universe of a thing of measurable
magnitude which is at the same time ever-abiding
and absolutely stable. And because the ultimate Being is stable, this Being, as Ātman or the ultimate
Self in man, is magnitudeless, is smaller than the

smallest. And because the Ātman in the individual is smaller than the smallest, is like a point (*anu*), we feel the Ātman to be nowhere, located at no definite spot, and yet, as it were, everywhere in the body. Ātman, the ultimate Self of man, seems to be present wherever attention, i.e. a particular mental function or movement, is directed.

At the same time, and paradoxical though it may seem, Ātman, as the abiding Being, is "greater than the great" (*mahato mahīyān*), that is, infinitely great. This is the reason why we can experience the universe as something spreading itself out in boundless space, and have also the feeling that we reach out even beyond the universe, beyond every limit which may be imagined in space. The ultimate Being in us seems to outrun the uttermost reaches of our senses.[4] It would be impossible to have these experiences, if Ātman were only "infinitely small," like, say, a mathematical point.

But it might be thought that, in order to have the experience of wide-reachingness in space, Ātman need not be infinitely great: a limited greatness (like the extent of the universe, which must, after all, be limited) would equally serve the purpose. This cannot be. For whatever is of limited extent and has therefore a measurable magnitude is, as noted above, perishable and cannot be abiding. But Ātman is abiding Being; Ātman, therefore, besides being infinitely small, must also be infinitely great; or, as the Vedic texts have it, Ātman is both "smaller than the small" and "greater than the great." That is to say, Ātman is beyond all space, everywhere and nowhere.

Furthermore the ultimate Being is not an unconscious, unintelligent Being; on the contrary, the ulti-

---

[4] Cf. *tad dhāvato 'nyān atyeti tishthat* and *nainad devā āpnuvan pūrvam arshat* (Īshā Upanishad 4).

mate Being is Awareness (*chit*) itself. Because the
ultimate Being is awareness, and because this Being
is the real and ultimate experiencing subject in an
individual, the latter is *aware* of anything objective,
whether through the senses or only mentally. Awareness is felt, in experience, to belong to what abides
in us as the ultimate ground of our existence and not
to anything else which, even though a purely mental
fact, can yet be experienced as something other than
the Self, the experiencing subject.

The Being as Ātman is also feeling. Feeling is the
very root and ground of our existence as conscious
entities. And this feeling is joyousness (*ānanda*);
to live and to be is joy; suffering is only when we
are not able to live and to be as we would. Suffering
is not the essential nature of Being, but joy (*ānanda*)
is; it is joy that is the root of all love and peace and
bliss.[5]

Thus Ātman, the ultimate Self in man, is pure
Being (*sat*), objectless Awareness (*chit*), and un-
clouded Joy (*ānanda*).

And Ātman, the ultimate Being, is timeless and
spaceless.

As such, the ultimate Being is only one Being
(*ekam sat*), one Ātman in all individuals. There
cannot be many ultimate Beings, many Ātmans.
Plurality has meaning only when there is any division either in time or space, or in regard to attributes.

In regard to attributes, the ultimate Being of one
individual entity cannot in any way be distinguished
from the ultimate Being of a different individual.

---

[5] That *ānanda* means also "love" will be clear if we recall that
the word is sometimes rendered by *priti,* and is, in one form of
its manifestation in the individual, sexual pleasure, the function
of *upasthendriya.* Cf. also Brih. Up. 4.3.21, where the supreme
and final experience of realizing Brahman is likened to the feeling of being embraced by the beloved woman and of forgetfulness
of all else in that enjoyment. The feeling of *ānanda* is further
described as *svarūpa-vishrānti,* absolute rest in oneself, that is
to say, *ānanda* is peace.

The ultimate ground in one case is just as pure Being, Awareness, and Joy as in the other. Distinctions and differences in the attributes of individual subjects are caused only by the objective contents of experience, by what comes to be placed, as it were, in front of the pure Being and Awareness and seems to color the feeling of pure Joy. There can therefore be no distinction in regard to attributes between the Ātman in one individual and that in another.

Nor can there be any division in Ātman in regard to time and space. There can be no meaning in the statement that there are, *in different places,* different Ātmans, all absolutely alike in regard to attributes and all infinitely great, i.e. all equally occupying every conceivable space, or, which is the same thing, all equally beyond every space limitation. It is equally meaningless to say that, while Ātmans are all ever-abiding, there existed in the past some Ātmans that have ceased to exist now, or that, while there are now other equally ever-abiding Ātmans, they too will cease to exist in the future. Thus there is but one ultimate Being that is the one common ground, one Ātman, one undivided Self, in every separate individual and in the universe.

This is held *not* as a matter of mere inference, but as a positive fact of experience on the part of men called Yogins and Rishis, who, it is maintained further, have been produced in an unbroken chain of succession down to this day, and whose positive experience and vision can be acquired by anyone, duly qualified, anywhere in any country and at any time. It is recognized, moreover, that this is the experience also of all true seers in other parts of the world who have been vaguely called "mystics."

This ultimate All-aware, All-joy Being, who is thus the Ātman, the ultimate Self, both of the individual and of the universe and everything in it, is in reality beyond all predicates and names, as he is beyond all strictly logical formulation in thought. As such he is referred to, in early Vedic texts, in a manner which is indefinite, no doubt intentionally. He is spoken of merely as "That One" and as the "One Being." But when a name is given to him, he is called Purusha, the Person; and in later literature Uttama-Purusha or, which is the same thing, Purushottama, the Supreme, the Ultimate Person.

He is also called Brahman, though, strictly speaking, this name should be confined, as will be seen later, to a particular aspect of Purusha, the Ultimate Person.

We thus get *apparently* two fundamental realities or principles:

(1) Purusha as the one ultimate, timeless and spaceless Being and Self of man and the universe; and

(2) The system of ever-changing movements which constitute the universe and whatever is ever experienced as an object, movements which are apparently other than, and antithetical to, Purusha, the unchanging Being.

In reality, however, the system of movements, as the root of objectivity, is not a separate independent reality at all, but only Purusha appearing in a second role, but without ceasing, even for a moment, to be the abiding, unchanging, and unmoving Being that He in himself is. Movement by itself, without something moving, has really no meaning. And what really moves, or rather appears to be moving, is only Purusha in another aspect—the aspect in which the endlessly enduring and the infinitely great, the timeless and spaceless Being appears, in the first instance, as the starting point of all that exists in time and space as well as of both time and space themselves. That is to say, he appears as the infinitely small, or, to use a later expression, as the "Benign Point" (*shiva bindu*). In other words, there is only one reality, only one principle, and that is Purusha; so that the root of objectivity is only Purusha in another phase, the phase of self-limitation, or, as it is called in the Vedas, the phase of "sacrifice" (*yajña*) —Purusha sacrificing himself ceaselessly by the ceaseless "negation" and the limitless "contraction" of his own timeless and spaceless Being, yet without suffering the least diminution or change in that ultimate Being that is himself.[6]

To put this in the language of the famous Purusha-Sūkta section of the Rig-Veda, the aspect in which he appears as the self-sacrificing source of the objective universe is, as it were, only a "quarter" of himself, while "three quarters of him" remain unmanifest beyond all objective thought and experience. That is to say, what of him appears as the universe is but a very limited aspect, while what remains unmanifest is unlimited, is incomparably great. That this is the real significance of the Rig-Vedic text—which might be misconceived as meaning that Purusha is capable of an actual division, so that one measurable part of him appears as the universe while three equally measurable parts lie beyond—will be seen from another verse of the Vedas, perhaps a later one, which endeavors to define this relation between the two aspects of Purusha in quite a different manner. In the form of a paradox, it declares:

> That which lies beyond is Plenum, [full and undiminished]. That which appears as this here [i.e. as the universal] is also Plenum, equally full and undiminished. Out from Plenum, Plenum arises. Plenum having been taken away out of Plenum, what remains is still the same [undiminished] Plenum. (Brih. Up. 5.1.)

---

[6] On this point, see the writer's *Kashmir Shaivaism*. *Avidyā* is really "negation" (*nishedha*) of Being, while *tamas* is "contraction" (*samkocana*).

The purport of this paradoxical statement is that Purusha, the timeless, spaceless Being, cannot possibly be really divided; the division of him, as unmanifest and manifest, is only apparent; and that Purusha in the aspect that becomes the universe is as full and complete as the aspect that transcends the universe and remains as ever undimmed and unchanged, without undergoing in any way any diminution whatsoever.

It is a state of affairs which cannot possibly be formulated in any logical statement whatsoever without contradiction. Hence it is often spoken of as "indefinable" (*anirvācya*). It can, however, be made intelligible, at least partially if not fully, by an example or two.

One such example may perhaps be found in the domain of biology, in the division of a single vital cell into many. Here each new cell appears to have the same amount of vitality as the original one, apparently without any diminution, even when the original cell is divided many times over.

Another illustration of the process may perhaps be furnished by what is called in psychology "dissociation of personality." In this case, each new personality seems to be as complete and self-consistent as the one from which it is produced, and which, at the same time, seems to remain in every way unaffected.

A third illustration will perhaps be found in the sphere of physics. According to this, ions and electrons would seem to be but "points of strain" or "energy units" in a storehouse of universal energy, whether this storehouse be regarded as "ether," as hitherto, or as something else. As a center and fountain of energy, each of these "energy units" would seem to be as inexhaustible as the entire storehouse from which it is produced.

But perhaps the best example of the relation between the ultimate Being and the manifestation of him is to be found in the relation between what is recognized by psychologists in the West, practically universally, as man's unconscious and his surface consciousness as a particular individual. The unconscious does not cease to exist as such when the surface consciousness has appeared. The surface conciousness behaves as though it were an entity quite apart from and independent of the unconscious, which, as a matter of fact, is its true being and ground. The two exist together as it were simultaneously, and while the surface consciousness has but little, if any, notion of its ground, the unconscious is fully aware of the former, which is, as it were, a child of the unconscious and for which the unconscious holds all that is "lost" and forgotten of the previous experiences as life of the individual, so that the "lost" memory of such experiences can be brought up to the surface consciousness by hypnotism and by yoga (to be explained later).

These are, however, only rough examples; and even if they represented quite a correct state of things in nature, they nevertheless could not be regarded as, in every respect, complete illustrations of the relation which subsists between the manifest and the unmanifest aspects of Purusha. In reality, this relation is one which, as said before, cannot be defined or described in any terms which will not be self-contradictory. Recognizing this limitation clearly, it may be said that it is one and the same Purusha, who in one of his aspects becomes the universe, while he yet remains entirely unchanged and undiminished in his true Being, which is the other aspect, away from and transcending the universe.

In his aspect as manifesting the universe, Purusha is given various names: usually in this aspect he is

called *Brahman,* a name which literally means the
Word and "He who grows great,"[7] so that the un-
manifest aspect has in later times been called Para-
Brahman, which should really mean what transcends
Brahman, the Word.

To the manifesting aspect of Purusha are also given
the names Īsh, Īsha, and Īshvara, all meaning
"Lord."[8]

Thus it is this Brahman, "Word," or Īsha, "Lord,"
who is really the Self, root, and origin of both the
individual and the universe. He, indeed, is the core
of all that is; and He is Ānanda—Joy and Bliss and
Love and Peace in one.[9] Hence do the Vedas proclaim:

From Ānanda, in truth, all Beings spring forth
into existence; by Ānanda, when born, they live;
and unto Ānanda they flee and enter. And
again:

Who, indeed, would move, who would
breathe, if there were not this Ānanda buried
in the inmost space of every heart. For He

---

[7] The word *brahman* is neuter only in form, not in meaning, in
the same way as for instance, *mitra,* "friend," is neuter, *dārāh,*
"wife," is masculine plural, and *kalatra,* "wife," is neuter, only
in form. Such expressions should be translated in reference to
their meaning and not according to their grammatical gender in
Sanskrit. It is absurd to refer to Brahman, the all-intelligent, all-
bliss, and ever-abiding Being, by the pronoun *it,* as though he was
something unintelligent and unfeeling. This has been the cause
of a great deal of misunderstanding as to what is really meant
by Brahman, who is, in strict truth, neither male nor female, and
certainly not an unintelligent neuter entity such as a stone, any
more than the real personality of a human being is either male,
female, or neuter. Brahman is derived from the root *brih,* "to
grow, to grow great," which is undoubtedly only *vridh* in another
form. If so, the English "Word" is ultimately the same as the
Vedic Brahman even etymologically.
[8] But literally perhaps "what spreads thread-like or net-like" all
over the universe and thus controls everything in it; Ishvara is
described as *jāla-vat,* "the net-wielder" or "made up of nets." The
technical names *sūtrātman,* "the Atman that spreads thread-like,"
and *antar-yāmin,* "the puller from within," may also be compared
in this connection.
[9] See footnote 5 above for the meaning of *ānanda.*

alone, standing there, makes all life joyous and happy and blissful and loving.

In other words, the universe, with everything in it, is only an outward flow and a crystallized form of the unceasingly upwelling Joy of Brahman.

But the present universe is not the only such manifestation. At some time in the past, no matter how remote, this universe came into existence, as surely as it shall end some day in the future, no matter how distant. Brahman, on the other hand, is timeless, an aspect of the timeless Purusha. He has existed at all times, or, which is the same thing, beyond all times. It cannot, therefore, be that while he had existed for all eternity without ever before manifesting a universe, he suddenly appeared as this universe at some point of time, which, however long past, was but yesterday as compared with the timeless existence of Brahman. It is quite irrational to imagine that, having remained, as it were, idle all those countless aeons, timeless times, Brahman suddenly became this universe. The truth, on the contrary, is that Brahman has gone on appearing as universes forever without a beginning, so that the present universe is but one in a beginningless series, in which each succeeding universe is, as it were, a reincarnation of a previous one that has perished.

Thus it happens that, as the Self of the universe, Brahman, like Purusha, has also a twofold phase:

(1) The phase of manifestation as the actual universe (this being called *shrishti,* "throwing out"; also *kalpa,* "imagining, or carving out") ;[10] and

(2) The phase in which the universe exists only in a potential form, just as the future tree exists in the seed (this being called *pralaya,* "absorption" or "dissolution") .

---

[10] The term *kalpa* is used also in the sense of a complete cycle of one phase of manifestation and one phase of potentiality.

It is between these two phases that Brahman, as the Self of the universe, has gone on alternating eternally, from beginningless time. The phase as an actual universe is a state of heterogeneous and multifarious objectivity, while the potential phase is a state of universal homogeneity, which is compared to an ocean, mighty and ever-flowing, but without a wave or ripple.[11]

The potential phase is also likened to a state of profound sleep, when Brahman, after his universe-working exertion, is, as it were, at rest. To use the Vedic language, describing one such sleep and rest, previous to the emergence of this present universe: "By His own nature did That One breathe, though not a breath of wind was blowing."[12]

And if Pralaya, the potential state of the universe, represents sleep on the part of Brahman, the fresh manifestation of a new universe is his waking-up anew, or, which is the same thing, the waking-up of Ātman as the Self of the Universe. Indeed, the successive stages (at least the first stages) through which Ātman passes, till the uttermost physical objectivity is reached, are not unlike the stages of the swift mental journey of an individual person imme-

---

[11] The state of potentiality is therefore referred to as *salila,* "the ever-moving water," *maho-arnas,* "the great flood," and *samudra arnava,* "the ocean in the flow." In the Purānas it is called *kārana-samudra* or *kārana-vāri,* "ocean of causes." In the Sānkhya it is Prakriti in the *pralaya* state in which there is but a *sadrisha-parināma,* i.e. homogeneous movement, a gentle internal but wave-less flow, as there may be in an ocean. Prakriti, which is really a "process," is always moving, never at rest. Only, when it appears as the actual universe it is still flowing, but, as it were, in a three-fold current, giving rise to all kinds od eddies, ripples, and waves, which are the diversified objects. But in *pralaya,* when there is only the *sadrisha-parināma,* there is but a uniform flow without any waves and ripples whatsoever.

May not this be the primeval Water of Thales? And may not the name Thales be a ploy on "sea"?

[12] RV. 10. 129.2: *ānid avātam svadhayā tad ekam,* lit. "breathed windless, by his own power, That One." The word *svadhā* is important. It means really what is called *svabhāva, māyā,* and *prakriti* in later writings.

diately on waking. This will be seen later when we come to consider how these stages come into existence. Let us, for the present, understand what they are. This can be done without much difficulty, because the stages, like the ultimate Being himself, are all present with us and always co-operating ceaselessly in every experience, however trivial, that we have in life.

Beginning at the physical—which is, as it were, the farthest removed from Ātman as he is in himself, and where, therefore, he is the most veiled—and without noticing intermediate steps in the process, the "stages" may broadly be counted as follows:

A. Two factors which are different from each other as facts of experience though not in essence, in much the same way as solids and liquids are different in experience, even though they may be *essentially* the same thing. These are:

(1) The Physical, which enters into the composition of our bodies, and also constitutes the material and basis of what we perceive through the bodily senses; this is known as the *bhūtas,* or, as built up into the body of a living entity, *anna,* food.

(2) The Vital, which holds together the Physical in living things as an organic whole and makes it behave like a living entity, as distinguished from the "dead," or from what is called the "inorganic"; this is named *prāna,* lit. "forthgoing," i.e. "responsive energy," "life."[13]

Of these again, the Physical is of two classes:

(a) A class of discrete entities, something like what physics calls "ions" and "electrons"; these are known as *paramānus* (the extremely, even infinitely, small things).

(b) A Continuum (or what looks like it), not

---

[13] The term *prāna* is usually rendered "breathing"; this, however, is only a function of *prāna.*

unlike the "ether" which is, or at any rate formerly was, postulated by physicists as a sort of universal medium and background of all physical phenomena. It is called *ākāsha*.[14]

The Paramānus would be practically identical with the ions and electrons of physics, if the latter were entities without a magnitude. Paramānus have "no inside and outside," and, when piled up so as to touch one another, produce only Paramānus. From this, it is clear that Paramānus are magnitudeless entities, practically like mathematical points; the ions and electrons of physics, on the other hand, have probably some magnitude—some length, breadth, and thickness—no matter how minute. It may not be impossible that modern physics may yet discover that ions and electrons, in case they have any magnitude, are only things derived, like atoms, from still simpler entities; and these latter, if magnitudeless, would then be the Paramānus as conceived from the Vedic point of view.

The other physical entity, the Continuum or Ākāsha, differs from the "ether" in that Ākāsha consists really of an infinite number of very rigid lines, called *dishah* (or, in the singular, *dish*), i.e. directions or pointers, which are figured in a different school of tradition as the "hair of Shiva."[15]

Of these again, it is the discrete Paramānus which, as stimuli moving and waving in various ways, are related especially to the four specific sensations of Temperature (heat and cold), Color, Flavor, and Odor. The Paramānus are therefore classed under

---

[14] For the probable derivation and literal meaning of *ākāsha*, see below.

[15] On this point, see the writer's *Kashmir Shaivaism*. The name *ākāsha* itself probably conveyed this idea originally, being most probably derived from *ā* = *samantāt*, "in all directions," and *kāsha*, "reed" or what looks like reeds. In various Vedic texts the universe is referred to as *yajña*, "sacrifice," which then is figured as something woven, as with threads. Cf. also the epithet *jālavat*, applied to Ishā, and the term *sūtrātman*, both mentioned above.

four heads:

> the Temperature-Stimuli
> the Color-Stimuli
> the Flavor-Stimuli
> the Odor-Stimuli

They, again, in various groupings of more or less close cohesion, are related especially to the experiences of hardness, softness, weight, solidity, liquidity, and the like. From this point of view they are respectively named symbolically, or at any rate technically, Air, Fire, Water, and Earth, which are the so-called four "elements" of the philosophy of India and Greece. These names, in the technical sense and insofar at least as the philosophy of India is concerned, do not signify—and this cannot be too strongly emphasized—Air, Fire, Water, and Earth *as ordinarily understood,* but just the four classes of stimuli giving rise to the four specific sensations mentioned above.[16]

While the discrete Paramānus are thus ultimately responsible for the four specific sensations named above, or, as already suggested, they are the inferred, i.e. the "imagined," origin of the four types of sensation-forms, it is the Continuum or Ākāsha which is similarly responsible for the sensation of sound as we perceive it ordinarily.[17] Sound is not the essential and inalienable property of any discrete object anywhere that we know and experience in the universe: every one of the discrete objects can be absolutely silent, but none absolutely unaffecting either as temperature, or color, or flavor, or odor, or as some combination of them. In other words, it is impossible to know any discrete objects whatsoever, except

---

[16] On this point, see the writer's *Hindu Realism* (section on Paramānus).

[17] For an explanation of the idea of Ākāsha being the basis and medium of sound, see the writer's *Hindu Realism* (section on Ākāsha).

through one or the other of these sensation-forms; on the other hand, they can all be known without sound. And that is because sound is not the essential property of any of these. Sound is related specially to Ākāsha, is ethereal. This need not seem absurd now, in view of the daily ·broadcasting of messages and music by means of what is certainly not any of the discrete forms of matter, but something ethereal.

As the ethereal Ākāsha fills all space, so that there is really no empty space in the absolute sense, the apparently empty spaces inside our bodies are full of Ākāsha, while the ponderable material therein is supplied by the four discrete groups of the Physical.

As regards the Vital (*prāna*), its nature and functions will be considered later.

The only point to be noted here, in regard to the Physical (the material) and the Vital, is that we have them both in us.

Similarly in regard to the other stages in the process of Ātman involving himself in objectivity; they are also in and with us always, in every experience of daily life, and may be enumerated as follows:

B.	(1)	The Sense-powers (Indriyas) in two groups:

   (a)	Those functioning through the nervous system; they may be called the Cognitive Senses (in Sanskrit, *jñānendriya*) ;

   (b)	Those functioning through the muscles; they may be called the Reactive Senses or the Muscular Senses (in Sanskrit, *karmendriya*) .

 (2)	Concrete Mentality (Manas)

 (3)	Sense-objects-in-general (Arthas, Bhūta-mātrās, or Tanmātras)

 (4)	The Ego-complex (Vijñāna, Buddhi, or Ahamkāra)

 (5)	The Universal Ideation (Mahat or Mahat Ātman)

(6) Nothingness (Asat, Avyakta, or Avidyā)

The Cognitive Senses are the five obvious powers, or capacities, of hearing, feeling temperature (heat and cold), seeing, tasting, and smelling; while the Reactive Senses are the capacities of voicing, handling (touching and pressing), and locomotion, and of the voluntary muscular movements of rejecting from the body various forms of matter, especially liquids and solids.[18]

The only point about them that we need to note here is that, in the Vedic view, those powers are not identical with the physical bodily organs which are generally employed for their functioning; and that the powers are really independent of the physical organs, and belong to what is, as will be seen later, something other than the physical, i.e to the limited "ego"; so that, when the particular physical organ by which one of these powers operates is damaged or destroyed, the latter can often still function in some other way. For instance, when the hand of a man is injured, he can yet handle things, say, by his feet.[19]

Concrete Mentality (*manas* in Sanskrit) is that which shows itself, in one of its functions, as attention, without the co-operation of which the senses cannot function. As attention it is also selective, in that it selects, out of the multifarious sensation-stimuli impinging ceaselessly upon us from every direction, a few, which are "attended to," while the others are excluded (*vyavacchidya mano lakshayati*), so that none but the selected group is transformed into a particular sensation or group of sensations. When, for instance, a person is watching a performance in a circus tent, let us say, in the middle of a busy town, and does not notice the noise of traffic

---

[18] The act of taking such things into the body is partly the function of Hastendriya (Power of Handling) and partly of Prāna (Vitality).

[19] On this point see the writer's *Kashmir Shaivaism*.

outside, it is not that the sound-stimuli from the streets are not pouring in upon him; but those stimuli are not being transformed in him into sound-forms, because his Concrete Mentality (Manas) has excluded them at the time and has fixed itself as attention on that particular group of stimuli which are being transformed as the circus performance that is being observed.

Concrete Mentality, moreover, is also that which, in addition to selecting a particular group or groups of sense-stimuli, builds up "concrete" sense-forms or images—visual, auditory or otherwise—out of the stimuli so selected.[20] It is this Concrete Mentality (Manas) in the absence of which a person is absent-minded, so that he fails to notice an object even when it is, as it is said, right before him. Thus the presence in us of this Concrete Mentality (Manas) is quite obvious in every act of sense perception.

The presence in us, or in relation to us, of the next group, the Sense-objects-in-general, is somewhat difficult to detect. They may, however, be inferred, as the standards to which constant references are made whenever we experience a sensation, such as a sound or a color or any other. We experience these only as particulars—as one variety among others, all belonging to a general class. Thus, in the matter of color, what we actually perceive are the varieties red, blue, yellow, and the like, which are all so different from one another. Yet we regard them all, as it were instinctively, as of the same class, color-in-general. Of color-in-general, however, we have no direct experience anywhere in our ordinary life; nor can we picture vividly to ourselves this color-in-general or any other sensation-in-general. Yet there must be somewhere, in or in relation to some part

---

[20] Manas has as its function *samkalpa* and *vikalpa*, besides *vya-vaccheda*.

of our individual being, this color-in-general and every other sensation-in-general; otherwise they could never be thought of. The exact nature of this relation will be considered later. All we need to note here is that the sensation-generals do exist somewhere. The Yogins maintain that they are directly and positively experienced when a certain stage in the unfoldment of the superconscious in man is reached by means of the true yoga discipline.[21]

The next item, the Ego-complex or simply the ego, the limited "I," is that factor in us as individuals which, as one of its functions, supplies all that is needed to substantiate a sensation-form—as what is actually "given" by a sense or senses—so as to make of it a particular object. Thus, for instance, when we say we see a red rose from a distance, what is actually given at the moment by the sense of sight is nothing but a stream of red color points, made into the form of a rose by the operation of the Concrete Mentality (Manas). And it is, therefore, not yet what we really mean by a red rose, which is not only

---

[21] The question of the origin of things abstract can never be finally decided for everybody by merely inferential reasoning. Inferentially the abstract will be always regarded by some as things produced and built up gradually from elements supplied by experiences of the concrete; while others will hold, equally rationally, that they are latent, innate in us, and that the experiences of the concrete only provide the occasion for their coming out into play. Speculative or inferential reasoning by itself can never satisfy all persons equally in regard to any question even when they are equally intellectual. There will always be Deweys and Bertrand Russells, Eddingtons and Whiteheads, who will never be all agreed fully on any question on merely inferential grounds. *Naishā tarkena matir āpaneyā*, "By mere argument this truth [about the transcendental] cannot be reached." The function of what in India corresponds to the philosophy of the Occident is not, therefore, to *discover* truth of the abstract and the transcendental, but only to discuss the rationality or otherwise of what is *given* as statements embodying positive experiences of the transcendental (only *vicāra* on what is given as *shruti*). For it is held in India that all transcendental truth, no matter how abstract, can be directly and positively experienced by duly qualified persons by means of yoga (of the right kind, of course). (The Vedānta-sūtra equivalent of *naishā tarkena matir āpaneyā*, Katha 2.9, is *tarkāpratishthānāt*, Vedānta-sūtras 2.1.11.)

the red color we actually see but also several other attributes associated with, and, as it were, placed under, the color-form as its supporting frame, its substance. These are, for instance, the attributes of softness, coolness, light weight, fragrance (which, let us suppose, we are not actually smelling at the time, being far away from the rose), and the like. A rose means all these and much more and not merely the patch of color we actually see. And as we associate them with what is actually given by the sense of sight at the time, they are really brought out from some part of our being; and we can so bring them out only because they are stored there as facts of actual experiences of all these attributes of the rose, experiences gained not merely by seeing roses from a distance, but by handling and smelling them. The part of our nature where these and similar other facts of concrete experiences are held together—arrogated, retained as one's own—is the ego, which is nothing but a "bundle" of the actual experiences of things concrete kept cohering together by the feeling of "my and mine."

Its Vedic name, *vijñāna,* i.e. various bits of experiences (*jñāna*) held together as an organic whole and unit, is thus quite appropriate. In the Sankhya and most other post-Vedic writings it is called Ahamkara, the "Ego-Creature,"[22] the ego as something created and built up.

The presence of the next item is revealed in the positive and emphatic judgment (*buddhi*): "This is a rose, not anything else." Such a judgment is possible not only because we are able to refer the

---

[22] This is also the *vijñāna* (one of the five Skandhas) of Buddhist philosophy. In the Katha Upanishad it is referred to by the additional names of *jñāna-ātman,* i.e. Ātman of limited individual experience, and *buddhi,* Intelligence and Reason. The term *buddhi,* however, is used in the Sānkhya as an alternative name for *mahat,* to be considered next. The Sānkhya use of *buddhi* as a technical term is the more usual practice.

particular rose now before us—having been built in the way mentioned above—to the ideal rose, and to the ideal flower, i.e. to rose as a class and to flower as a class, but also to the class not-rose, i.e. to everything else in the universe other than the ideal rose. This means there is something in us which is universal and, however unconscious, is always present. This something provides as the standard of reference not only the ideal rose and the ideal flower but also the ideal everything. It is to this ideal standard that an instant reference is made when the present rose is recognized as belonging to the class "rose" and to the class "flower" and, finally, as outside the whole of the remaining universe.

This universal standard of reference, which is really a great and universal ideation of everything possible, enabling us to form a positive judgment, is called Mahat, "the Mighty," or Mahat Ātman, "the Mighty Self," of our individual lives.

The final factor, or stage (final when counted up from the Physical but first from the standpoint of a new universal manifestation) is the Power of Negation. It shows itself as ever present with us not only when we form a positive judgment of the type mentioned above, but as the power which sends us to sleep every day of our lives and ceaselessly obliterates things and objects from our view, so that none can remain forever before our gaze as limited entities, even though our inmost Self, our ultimate Being, is Awareness itself, boundless, timeless, and spaceless. On the other hand, if it were not for this Power of Negation ceaselessly operating in us there would be no endeavor and no movement in life, which from the Vedic point of view is but a ceaseless seeking of that Joy (Ānanda) of which we have somewhere had a foretaste, but which is now lost, taken away, suppressed, and wrought into Nothing by this Power of Negation.

It shows itself in a positive and emphatic judg-ment, such as "this is a rose and nothing else," in-sofar as this judgment involves the negation, suppres-sion, and putting away from experience of everything else but the rose, the "everything" here being consti-tuted by the Universal Ideation considered above.

These then are the stages—counted in the reverse order—of Ātman's march away from his own true state until his appearance as the Physical is reached. And they are all contained in every one of us, consti-tuting the various factors of our individual existence. Thus:

The Physical constitutes the physical body.

The Vital (Life), the Sense Powers and Sensation-generals, the Concrete Mentality (Manas) and the Ego constituting what is generally called the individual soul—that which differentiates one individual from another in character, mentality, and the like (Subtle Typical Body, the *sūkshma-deha* or *lingadeha* of the Darshanas).

The Universal Ideation as synthesizing and uni-fying, i.e. bridging all gulf of separation, is what is later termed the Causal Body (kāranadeha), that which makes us love and feel ourselves as one with all; it may perhaps be said to corre-spond to what St. Paul calls spirit in his three-fold division of man into body, soul, and spirit.

The Principle of Negation, or Sacrifice or rather self-sacrifice, is, as will be seen later, the same as Shabda-Brahman, the Universal sound-Word, and its presence in us will be explained later. It may be said to correspond to the Logos or the Christ Principle of Christian teaching.

Finally the Abiding Being stands as the background of all experience as the one ultimate Self in us all.

Counted in the order of their coming out into existence, these stages or principles, constituting the body, soul, spirit, and the divine in us, may be stated as follows:

(1) Nothingness (Asat, Avyakta, Avidyā, Ajā, Māyā in the Vedas; Prakriti, Pradhāna, and Shakti in the Sānkhya and the Tantras).

(2) Universal Ideation, or simply Ideation, or the Ideal (Mahat, Mahat Ātman).

(3) Ego-Creature or ego, i.e. the bundle of concrete experiences held together as an organic unit, and behaving as such, felt as the local and temporal "I"—as "I am now here," "I am John Smith" (Vijñāna, Ahamkāra).

    (a) Concrete Mentality (Manas)
    (b) Sensation-Generals (Bhūta-Mātrās; Tanmātras)
    (c) Sense-Powers (Indriyas)
    (d) The Vital (Prāna)

(4) The Physical Bhūtas, the "Have-becomes," as the last things in the process of becoming limited.[23]

---

[23] This numbering is, of course, only according to one particular method of classification. The stages are greater or less in number according as several intermediate stages are counted as independent ones or not. In the Taittirīya Upanishad, for instance, the *Bhūtas* are declared at once as coming out of Ātman without a mention of any of the antecedent stages in the process.

It may be noted here that the scheme of Buddhist Nidānas, twelve in number ("Causal Nexus") is only another way of presenting the same process (see the writer's *Great Origination*). The later attempts, Ceylonese and otherwise, to interpret the Nidānas without reference to the antecedent and closely allied Upanishadic and Sānkhya thought have resulted in almost childish absurdities. The Buddha repeatedly declared that he only reproclaimed the ancient "Arya Dharma." The garb of it alone was somewhat new—not completely. In the case of the Nidānas, several of them are identical even in name with some of the stages named above; while others are easily recognizable as identical in meaning, though differing in names. The Nidānas are twelve in number because the Buddha counts certain intermediate stages as independent ones, between the Indriyas with Manas (taken together as Shad-Āyatanas) and the Physical, while he leaves out Prāna and includes Bhūta-mātrās in Nāma-Rūpa.

The chief difficulty lies in the supposed denial by the Buddha of an abiding, timeless and spaceless, ultimate Being. But let

And they come about in something like the following manner.[24]

Waking up, as it were, from his long slumber in the state of universal homogeneity (*pralaya*), Ātman "glances round" (*īkshati*), so to say, and finds nothing existing,[25] quite forgetful of the fact that he himself is. It may be compared to the experience of a

----

such doubters read carefully the epithets used by the Buddha to describe Nirvāna; they will then see that Nirvāna *is* this ultimate Being—Nirvāna being spoken of as Deathless (*amrita*), Bliss (*sukha*) and Endless Awareness (*anantam vijñānam*), Unborn (*ajāta*), Uncreate (*akrita*), and Uncompounded (*asamskrita*).

Nirvāna is the background of all experience; except for Nirvāna there would be no experience at all, declares the Buddha, and no escape from limited experience. See the statement on Nirvāna attributed to him in the Udāna (8.1 and 3).

The other difficulty in establishing the true relation between the teachings of the Buddha and of the Veda is the equally supposed notion that the Buddha denied continuity of the individual after death. As a matter of fact the Buddha's teaching in this respect is identical with the Vedāntic, namely continuity of identity in the midst of ceaseless change. Because of this only, one could call back to memory, according to both Buddhism and Vedic Philosophy, all the details of one's past existences during thousands, even millions, of years.

As for the Vedic Devas, the so-called "gods," the Buddha declared he was seeing them always and everywhere, even though invisible to most other people; and Buddhists, even of Ceylon, pray to them every day of their lives, as they make daily offerings to the Buddha. Compare the daily prayer of the Ceylonese and other Southern Buddhists not only to gods of the sky and earth, but also to Nāgas and other unseen entities (*ākāshatthā ca bhummatthā nāgā devā mahiddhikā*); Vishnu is the presiding deity in many a Buddhist monastery and temple. (Notice, for instance, the painted figure of Vishnu immediately on entering the Shrine of the Buddhist Vihāra built a few years ago in Calcutta by Anagārika Dharmapāla, of Ceylon.)

In fact there is not a statement attributed to the Buddha in the whole of the Pāli Suttas—supposed to be the oldest record of Buddhist teachings—which goes against any of the fundamental ideas of the Vedic Philosophy. Buddha denounces only the abuses of, and wrong values and interpretation put on the Vedas. But so does the Bhagavad-Gītā, a most orthodox and authoritative work on the Vedānta. Even the Upanishads, themselves parts of the Veda, regard large sections of it as inferior (*aparā*).

[24] For a fuller statement of this process, see the writer's *Kashmir Shaivaism*.

[25] What is called *avidyā* is only the experience "nothing is known" (*na vidyate kim api*), which again is the same as "nothing is." Thus *avidyā* is the equivalent of *asat*.

man who, let us say, went to sleep at a place which
was then full of things, but now is completely empty
of them, and who wakes up on this emptiness. His
first thought on waking is *not* himself, but the emptiness around him. In much the same way, Ātman beholds *not* himself but Nothingness, to which he
glances round. This glancing round on the part of
Ātman now, and experiencing Nothingness, is the
"Primary Deliberation" (*para vimarsha*); it is the
first fluttering, waving, vibrating Thought (*prathama spanda*); and, as a vibrating, waving Thought-
Energy, it is also the Primary Word (*brahman*),
the Primary Sound (*shabda*), and Name (*nama*). Forgetful as Ātman is of himself at this stage, it is an
act of self-negation (*nishedha-vyapara*); and self-
sacrifice (*yajña*) on his part—an act of great strength
and might (*shakti*). It is this, therefore, which most
probably constitutes what is called in Christianity
the Logos, or the Christ principle, which is really
a principle of self-sacrifice and love.

But this very experience of Nothingness leads to
the next stage, which is that of calling up before his
ever-aware gaze all that was in the past, i.e. the universe as it existed before. This now rises up as a
"Mighty Vision."[26]

It is likened, in the Sānkhya writings, to the
thought-experience of objectivity on waking up from
sound sleep (*suptotthita-cittavat*) on the part of an
individual such as mentioned earlier, namely, one
who went to sleep in the midst of a scene of beautiful
objects of infinite variety but now on waking finds
it quite empty. As he glances round and beholds
emptiness, he naturally remembers all that there was
before. It is in a manner somewhat like this that the
experience of the previous universe rises up as a

---

[26] This visioning stage is therefore called *pashyantī* in schools
of tradition other than the Vedic.

Mighty Vision at the stage we are now considering. At the same time it is a vision of what is to be; and therefore the pattern, complete and perfect, of the universe that is to appear presently in space and time. Hence it is the Ideal and the Archetypal, a Vision of Beauty (*rūpa*, which also means color and form).

While this survey of the ideal universe is going on—Ātman being thus far quite forgetful of himself, lost in the contemplation of the Universal Vision— the latter fades away, disappears, from his view by the operation of the negating energy which, as we have seen, is always present. This disappearance of the Vision leads Ātman to turn to *himself* as the Experiencer of the Vision, even though it is no longer there. Thus a distinction between himself as the Experiencer, the subject, and the Vision as the experienced object, arises for the first time; and by this very distinction, thus realized, Ātman becomes limited, regarding himself as something *other* than the Vision—becomes, as it were, one of two things, which means limitation and no longer the unlimited all-in-all. In other words, Ātman now becomes the limited I, the individual ego. This experience is also one of *movement* away from the Vision and then again toward it in search of it; that is to say it is Karma (activity, movement to and fro).

With these three—Name and Form (Word and Beauty, *nāma* and *rūpa*) previously mentioned, together with Karma—we get all the fundamentals of our experience of the objective universe.

Before proceeding further, however, with our brief description of the Process, which in the systematized Vedānta is called *vivarta*, "rolling out," it may be well to note here an important point in connection with the appearance and disappearance of the various phases of experience. It is this: that "disappearance" here does not mean absolute destruction or absolute nonexistence. On the contrary, in regard to these stages, the same principle holds good as in the relation between the unmanifest (transcendent) and the manifest (immanent) Purusha. We have noted above how, in the Vedic view, the unmanifest does not cease to be, even when the manifest comes out into existence. They both are, as it were, simultaneously. Following the same principle, even when Nothingness (*asat, avyakta*) comes into existence, Ātman exists also, though, as it were, on a different plane, and, so to say, unnoticed by Nothingness. Nothingness, or, which is the same thing, the Awareness of the Nonexistence of anything, is as much an entity as—indeed, more so than—an individual man is, both being, so to speak, equally ensouled by Ātman. As a matter of fact, all the stages are, as it were, so many entities, all conscious and feeling, though in varying degrees. As conscious entities, they are given appropriate names, such as Hiranyagarbha, Prajāpati, Prajñātman, Prajñānātman, Prājña, Sūtrātman, Shakti, and the like.[27]

And all these stages or entities exist, as it were, simultaneously, but in different planes, because conditions of time and space are not the same everywhere, as will be seen later. Simultaneity, therefore, cannot have the same meaning in regard to the relation of one stage to another as it has with respect to the mutual relations of facts and factors in one and the same stage. The stages exist, rather, in different space-time frames, to borrow an expression from the language of Relativity. Moreover, while there can be no subsequent stage in existence unless all the anterior stages exist, informing and ensouling the subsequent stage, as it were, yet every anterior stage can exist without what comes after it. Thus there

---

[27] From this point of view they correspond to some of the nine Sattāvāsas of the Buddhist teaching.

can be no physical stage without all the antecedent ones existing as its ground or soul. The stage of Nothingness, on the contrary, can exist without there being any of the subsequent appearances. In the same way, Brahman or Purusha can and does always exist in his true state, even without Nothingness or the universe. But the universe, from Nothingness onward, can never be without Purusha as the uttermost ground.

Thus it happens that when, by the operation of the Power of Negation (existing and working, as it were, from within), the Universal Vision vanishes from the view of Ātman and he becomes the limited Ego, the Vision, like Nothingness and Purusha, does not cease to exist, but continues in its own plane.

The Ego, the limited I, therefore, begins again to seek out[28] this lost, but unconsciously existing, Vision. The Vision can, however, no longer appear as a whole, as in the previous stage when the experiencing subject is one and ndivided with the Vision in every part and aspect.   can now be remembered and pictured back only in parts and bits and in different facets, inasmuch as the ego can see it only as an outside observer, and, as it were, from particular angles and therefore never as a whole Vision, never in all its dimensions.

And these bits and facets of the universal Vision, as they appear before the seeking ego, become the "sensations-in-general" or "sensation-generals" (bhū-tamātrā) out of which, as will be seen presently, the fully diversified and completely objectified universe is built up.

These sensation-generals are only five, as stated above, namely:

Sound-in-general (i.e. Sound undifferentiated)

---

[28] The dominant mood at this stage is *eshanā*, "seeking," desiring, willing; and what is found by seeking is *artha*, "thing desired and sought."

    Temperature-in-general
    Color-in-general
    Flavor-in-general
    Odor-in-general

They are all produced from the ego, drawn out, as though from its unconscious depths, as facets of the lost Universal Vision.

These sensation-generals are, as said above, the standards to which, in everyday life, an instant reference is made, as soon as one senses a particular variety of sound, temperature, color, flavor, or odor. They are, as we may say, the general concepts of these diversified and particularized sensations and cannot ordinarily be pictured to our mind, any more than there can be pictured, let us say, triangularity or humanity or kindness, in regard to which we call up only *particular* concrete images—particular triangles, particular human beings, particular acts of kindness, and the like—when we imagine we are picturing these things in themselves in their general abstract forms. In reality, we are in touch with the sensation-generals in a deeper part of our nature as individuals than in the purely physical world. And they come into existence, in the way described above, prior to the physical.

But as they come into existence, they also draw out from the ego the corresponding capacities or powers with which they are apprehended, i.e. they draw out the senses, or rather sense-powers. Indeed, the sensation-generals may be said to be but one end of a single composite phenomenon of which the sense-powers (*indriya*) represent the other side.

Corresponding to the sensation-generals, therefore, the sense-powers are, as mentioned before, also five:
    the power of hearing
    the power of sensing temperature
    the power of seeing

the power of tasting
the power of smelling

We may call them, as suggested above, by the general name of "cognitive senses" or "cognitive powers" (as a translation of the Sanskrit term *jñānendriya*).

With the appearance of these, there are also brought into existence, out from the ego, the powers of reacting on what is apprehended by means of the cognitive senses.

These powers of reacting or powers of action (designated in Sanskrit by the term *karmendriya*) are similarly five, as said before, namely: the power of voicing (as the reaction to hearing sound) ; the power of touching, i.e. putting one's hand, as it were, on the spot where the sensation of heat or cold or a tickling sensation is felt (reaction to temperature sensation) ; the power of locomotion, i.e. running away from or toward what appears suddenly as an objective vision (reaction to seeing color) ; and the two muscular efforts to eject from the physical body liquid, solid, and other forms of physical materiality. Reactive powers express themselves, in all instances, as muscular efforts, including the effort of "pressing," giving rise to the experience of hardness, softness, and the like, as said before. The reactive powers thus correspond, in certain of their aspects, to what is known as the muscular sense in psychology as it is studied in the Occident.

Along with these various sense-powers, both cognitive and reactive, there appears also from the Ego another power which is the most general of them all and without which not one of them can function, namely Manas, or the Concrete Mind, considered above. As already pointed out, it shows itself constantly as the power which, co-operating with one or other of the sense-powers, selects at a given moment only certain of the streams of impacts pouring in upon us from all directions of the objective world, and, excluding others, makes of the selected impacts the various sensation-forms of which we are directly aware, i.e. which constitute the actually "given" of the senses, in regard to any particular form of perception. It is really a movement, a waving to and fro, of the seeking here and there (*eshanā,* desire), which is the Manas, Concrete Mentality, when the movement assumes the form of an entity (a particle as the Vaisheshika views it), in much the same way as the ultimate constituents of physical matter are now regarded by science as simultaneously both waves and particles.

The next item to be considered is Vitality, or Prāna. It is what differentiates, in experience, the living from the nonliving. We may therefore call it simply Life.

This Life has, in the Vedic view, a fivefold function:

> Appropriation (*prāna*) [29]
> Rejection or Elimination (*apāna*)
> Assimilation (*samāna*)
> Distribution (*vyāna*)
> Regeneration (*udāna*)

The four first-named functions are obvious. As long as there is Life in the body these are continually going on. To begin with, Life is a selective process. It appropriates, takes into the system a certain quantity of material which it needs for building up and maintaining the organism in which it operates. It also rejects from the system what is not useful. One of the manifestations of this double activity of Life is seen in the ceaseless processes of breathing in and breathing out, which have therefore been taken as the most characteristic feature of life and even re-

---

[29] It should be noted that the term *prāna* is used in a twofold sense, both to signify life in general and as the name of a particular function of it.

garded as the equivalent of Life (Prāna). What is
selected is further *assimilated* to that form (as for
instance, blood) in which it can be built into the
system. This activity is compared to that of fire,
namely combustion, so that the result is said to rise
up like a sevenfold flame. The fourth function is
also apparent in that the assimilated material, such
as blood, is distributed all over the body, by means
of channels radiating from the heart[30] to every part
of the body.

The fifth type of function will require a little explanation. In one form, it is what serves as a link
between the Life in the individual and the Life universal, which, as explained below, is Brahman. It
is therefore said, metaphorically, that in dreamless
sleep, produced by the operation of the self-negating
Māyā, a person is "taken up daily to Brahman,"[31]
so that he thereby has his tired vitality refreshed, or,
as one might say, regenerated. This is done by re-
plenishing, as it were, our individual tanks of Life
from Brahman, the universal ocean of Life, when,
as in dreamless sleep, all diversified objectivity vanishes from our consciousness, and thus outlets of life
in us are for the time being largely shut off.

That function of Life which thus, as it were, carries us up to Brahman and enables us to have our
stores of Life daily regenerated is the fifth function,
called *udāna,* the "upgoing."

It also appears in another form, in the process of
what is known as reincarnation of the soul (as defined above), in that it carries what is really the
individual in us (apart from our physical bodies),
as our soul is, from one sphere of existence into another, from one death to a new birth. In the Vedic
view the individual in man, his individual soul, is,

---

[30] See Prashna Upanishad 3.6.
[31] Cf. Prashna Upanishad 4.4: *ahar ahar Brahma gamayati.*

it may be repeated, only the group of ever-changing factors, from ego downward to Life, held together as a unit against, as it were, the background of the one universal Being, the one ultimate Self in all. But though ever-changing, this group still maintains a certain self-identity and continuity, so that it can be felt and spoken of as the *same* entity in spite of the change, in much the same way as the physical body, although ceaselessly changing, can be still spoken of as one and the same body unit between birth and death. The only difference is that while the body is produced at birth (or conception) and perishes at death, the soul associated with a particular body comes into existence long before the body—the soul having been created by the process of manifestation in the way described—and continues to exist, even after the death of the body, as one and the same entity in the sense defined above. This type of self-identity and continuity is maintained by the soul even when not connected with a physical body and, as it were, floating in space between a death and new birth, in much the same way as a piece of music, broadcast into space, maintains its self-identity and individuality even when rushing through the ether (or whatever the medium may be called) so that it can be reproduced as the same music by means of a suitable receiver. The soul of man, in this sense and thus maintaining its self-identity, is born and dies again and again, until it reaches a stage in which that aspect of the ultimate Being standing behind the soul as its ground and, as it were involved in it— having forgotten himself in the way described above— reminds himself and ceases any longer to identify himself in feeling with the soul. When this state is reached, the soul perishes just as a particular body does at death. This is the state of experience when the self-forgetful Being, recollecting himself in a positive experience, realizes and proclaims the truth "He am I," "I am the Divine."[32] Until this experience, called Release or Freedom (*moksha*), is gained, the "soul" is born again and again; and as this takes place, it is carried from one state of existence into another by means of Life functioning in the fifth way as Udāna.[33]

In other words, death and rebirth of the soul are regarded as only different forms of the same phenomena of dreamless sleep and waking up which occur in the everyday life of the individual; and the movement to and fro in connection with both groups of phenomena is accomplished by the soul by means of Life functioning in its regenerative mode, which is Udāna.

This Life is therefore given a very important place in the Vedic view of things. Indeed, it is often identified with Ātman and Brahman, while it is spoken of in one place as coming into existence from Ātman directly without the intervention of any other stage and is regarded as having the same relation to Ātman as the shadow has to a man's body. Besides all things are said to be established in Life. Life is, in other words, the same as Brahman, the Universal Word or Sound, and the same movement as the latter.[34] But insofar as it operates in the individual, it comes into manifestation after the appearance of Manas, the Concrete Mentality, because it is Manas which as a seeking principle (*eshanā*) is the seat of desire, attention, and interest, and because it is by an unconscious act of this desire, attention, and interest that

---

[32] Compare the Christ-experience "I and my father are one."
[33] Cf. Prashna Upanishad 3.7-12.
[34] Cf. the *prathama spanda,* the first vibrating movement of Shiva Tattva in Trika Philosophy. Compare also the Gospel of John, 1.3-4, where life is identified with the Word. Life is a "waving" movement, like that of the flutter of a flag in the wind. Compare Rig-Veda 1.1.10 and note the play therein on *ketu* and *chit* and *dhī.*

Life functions in an individual and his body. For this reason we are told that Life comes into this body by the operation of the Manas.[35] For the same reason also we are further told that when a man learns, by means of yoga, to remove even his unconscious desire for and interest in the body, he can die at will, just as he can keep the body alive as long as he desires.[36]

With the appearance of Life, as it operates in the individual, we have reached the stage in the process of manifestation where we find all the elements of the superphysical universe, the realms of what is called the Spirit and the Soul, are ready. We have now to consider only the final step wherein the Physical is produced. We have seen that the Physical consists of the ethereal, all-pervading Ākāsha as the medium of Sound and four other groups of stimuli connected with the four sensations of Temperature-feeling (heat and cold), Color, Flavor, and Odor, symbolically called Air, Fire, Water, and Earth. These are collectively the five Bhūtas and are produced from the five sensation-generals, called Bhūta-mātrās (later Tanmātras), inasmuch as they have no other meaning except the inferred, i.e. the imagined origins or concomitants, moving or stationary, of the sensations of Sound, Temperature, Color, Flavor, and Odor as they are actually perceived by means of the senses operating in the physical body, i.e. as varieties of these sensations as distinguished from the general ones. And they are produced in the following manner.[37]

---

[35] Cf. Prashna Upanishad 3.3.

[36] Compare the "death-at-will" of Bhīshma. Several cases are quoted even in modern times as examples of "death-at-will" by simply withdrawing life from the body by an act of Manas.

[37] In none of the Vedic texts proper is this last step clearly explained, nor even any suggestion given, as in most of the other steps explained above, as to how the Bhūtas appear from the Bhūtamātrās, unless we take as such a suggestion the *trivritkarana* of Chāndogya Upanishad 6.3.3-4, which is a foreshadowing of the *pañcīkarana* idea. But the interpretation given here is traditional and quite old and in this sense authentic.

Prior to the appearance of the Physical, the objects of experience perceived by means of the senses which have already come into existence in the way described above are, as we have seen, of a general character, such as sound-in-general, temperature-feeling-in-general, color-in-general, and the like. There are as yet no variations in them. Owing, however, to the operation of the Principle of Negation (Asat, Avidyā) which is always present with the soul, they gradually cease to be noticed and then disappear altogether from experience, in much the same way as Universal Ideation (Mahat) disappeared from experience at an earlier stage when the limited I was produced. And just as then the Self, as it were, groped about in search of the vanished Universal, but found in its place only broken facets and fragments in the shape of the sensation-generals, in the same way the soul also, seeking in a similar manner to refind the lost generals, discovers in their place only bits and facets of them, because the Self as soul has now to work under a still further limitation, namely, that of Manas, the Concrete Mentality, which at this stage covers it up as in a cloak,[38] and makes it labor, as will be seen presently, under different conditions of space and time, in a different space-time frame. In other words, the sensation-generals, now being experienced through the medium of Manas, appear before the soul in their different variations as the one white sunlight appears in the many colors of the spectrum when seen through a prism, so that sound-in-general appears as varieties of sound, temperature-feeling-in-general as degrees of temperature, and the like.

And it is with the experience of these variations in the five general sensations that there also appear, as consequences, the five Bhūtas that we are now considering. For a proper understanding of these

---

[38] Sanskrit *kosha* or *kañcuka*.

stupendous consequences, let us place ourselves, in imagination, in a position similar to that in which the newly produced soul finds itself before it receives its first physical embodiment. We shall begin with the origin of Ākāsha, Ethereal Space.

But at the start let us make clear one very important point regarding certain fundamental characteristics of the Soul which, or rather who, is now a full-fledged Individual constituted of the previously produced Ego and Manas (Concrete Mentality), all the powers of sensation and action (*indriya*), and vitality (*prāna*).

He has also, buried within himself, as it were, not only Ātman, but also the previous stages of Nothingness (Asat, Avidyā) and Vision (Mahat), while the Ego is its central point, its nucleus and core. And they all show themselves as three well-defined tendencies or characteristics of the soul.

Of these, the ego (Ahamkāra) is really a principle of movement, having come into existence as the result of Ātman moving away, as it were, from the Vision (Mahat) to himself, as the subject of and distinguished from the Vision. And it shows itself constantly as such, i.e. as the tendency to run and jump about like a monkey.[39] This is called, in the technical language of systematized philosophy, Rajas (flaring up like red fire or dust).

Vision is the principle of *looking round,* it having come into existence by Ātman looking round, as it were, after the experience of Nothingness. This is later technically called Sattva (Existence).

Nothingness is the principle of negation, restriction, and contraction by which Purusha limits, restricts, contracts, and negates himself, as it were, so as to have the experience "Nothing is" (*na vidyate*

---

[39] It is actually symbolized by a monkey in the Buddhist scheme of the Nidānas, in which it corresponds to *vijñāna* as a *Skandha.*

kim api), forgetting even himself, forgetting that he is. This is later technically called Tamas (Darkness).[40]

After this necessary digression let us now consider the origin of Ākāsha, Ethereal Space. Let us imagine ourselves to be present face to face with, or rather to be immersed in, a sea of homogeneous sound which has already become, for the reason stated above, no sound at all, that it, has ceased to form an object of perception; and let us also imagine that there are no other objects whatsoever, as would be the case under the circumstances we are trying to picture, the other sensation-generals having equally and for equal reasons ceased to be perceived. Then let us further imagine that there suddenly arises, or, which

---

[40] Tamas, Sattva, and Rajas are spoken of in Vedic texts respectively as black (blue), white, and red (*Shvetāshvatara* Up. 4.5) and also by another figure, as food (*anna*), water (*ap*), and light (*tejas*) (Chāndogya Up. 6.4), and are later symbolized respectively (a) by blue in the throat of Shiva, who as destroyer of the universe is the embodiment of Tamas; (b) by the wheel-disk and wheeling Eagle (*garuda*) of Vishnu, who is the chief embodiment of Sattva; and (c) by the four faces—uttering forth words of creation in the four directions (meaning all directions) of Space— of the red Brahmā, who is the embodiment of Rajas. The names Tamas (Darkness), Sattva (Existence), and Rajas (Flaring up) are very significant and appropriate. It is obvious how the suppression of the All into Nothingness producing darkness, as it were, and the scattering around of everything into dust and thin air, as it were, are appropriately called Tamas and Rajas. The wheeling tendency is called Sattva, Existence, because, left to themselves, Rajas would scatter everything into atoms and ions, and Tamas would compress everything into Nothing. That is to say, by itself neither Rajas nor Tamas could keep anything existing as such a thing. It is the third tendency which by whirling things round ceaselessly within limited orbits—whether members of the solar system or particles constituting tiniest atoms—keep them existing (in Sanskrit, *sat*), whence the tendency is Sattva, "be-ness." This is undoubtedly the reason why *vartamāna,* literally whirling, means "existing," "present."

Tamas, Sattva, and Rajas—or, as they are generally enumerated in later literature, Sattva, Rajas, and Tamas—are the famous Gunas, lit. threads or strands which weave themselves into attributes of things or, which is the same thing, into the things themselves. They are the threads with which is woven the net that the Lord (Īsha) wields (*jālavat*). For a fuller account of the Gunas see the writer's *Kashmir Shaivaism.*

is the same thing, is suddenly perceived, a variety of sounds. What would be the experience that would instantly, instinctively, and necessarily follow this perception of a variety of sounds, as it were, all over the soul, as would now be the case, there being as yet no physical body and no localized senses—the senses being, as it were, all over the soul.

The answer from the Vedic point of view is that the consequent experience will be that of something going in *all directions* and filling the universe, i.e. Ethereal Space. In other words, with the experience of varieties in sound there is produced Ethereal Space. This happens in the following manner.

Simultaneously with the perception of varieties of sound, the soul will, under the influence of Rajas and working through Manas, at once *run out* everywhere, imagining that the perceived sounds are coming from all directions, corresponding to the experience of the sound as being all over the soul.

In other words there would be produced the notion of all directions imagined as straight, rigid lines going everywhere—imaginary lines no doubt, but very important ones.[41]

But, as we can learn from our daily experience, the mind and senses, even though sent out under the influence of Rajas, cannot run out for ever. The pull, from behind, of Tamas, also is always present in the soul. The mind therefore turns back after reaching a certain point in its outward run, and is compelled, owing to the centripetal pull of Tamas, to come back home to the center of the soul.

As it does so, however, it follows a course that is

---

[41] This need not startle anyone in the Occident in view of the fact that even scientific thinking as represented, for instance, by such a distinguished physicist and astronomer as Professor Eddington, is coming to realize that the universe is built up of "mind-stuff" and that the so-called "matter" is only "mind" in another shape, and produced from "mind"—"such stuff as dreams are made of."

curved and coiling, owing to the influence of Sattva. That this is how the mind works will be evident to any person endeavoring to concentrate the mind, i.e. to bring it to the central point of the soul. He will find that this cannot be done at once; the mind cannot be brought back, as it were, in a straight line. It hovers round for a time and then only comes to a rest either in concentration, if the soul is strong, or in sleep.

It thus happens that the mind, after ceasing to chase the sounds to the farthest possible limits of its running capacity, comes back to the soul by paths that, as it were, coil round the straight lines already produced by the outgoing tendency of Rajas.

The result is a most complicated structure. First there are these countless rigid straight lines going out in all directions—away from the soul as from a radiating center. For the soul, i.e. the limited Ātman, can move in all directions simultaneously even when related to a physical body; we can all verify this by listening to sounds all around us.

Second, these lines turn back after reaching a certain point on the outward run. These turning points thus constitute, for the soul that is spinning the lines out, the outer surface of his sphere of experience which is his universe.

Third, each of the returning lines, as they return, coil round the straight ones.

Thus the lines, straight and curved, produce in their totality a most complex structure—rather a marvelous piece of webbing. This fabric thus woven is the Ethereal Space and serves as the frame, the locale, in which all physical experiences of the particular soul are had. All objects experienced by the soul are held before him in different positional relations by the lines (*dishah*) of the Ethereal Space.[42]

---

[42] See the writer's *Hindu Realism,* pp. 54-61.

Though all imaginary, this Ethereal Space is for the soul very real and rigid and works, so long as it is not again transcended by yoga as explained below. And it is produced from the perception of variety in sensation of sound-in-general in the way explained.[43]

This picture of the inner structure of Ethereal Space is symbolized in various ways which it is not possible to explain here. There is, however, one particular form of symbolism which may be noted. It is that of the sacred Kusha grass. Quantities of this straight, line-like grass, representing the lines of living energy as the constituent elements of Ethereal Space, are spread on sacred sands, which again symbolize Ātman in his aspect as points constituting the lines. On the grass thus spread out there is lighted even now, in Brahmanical ceremonies, the sacrificial

---

[43] That the *dishah* are the essence of Ethereal Space and inseparably connected with "hearing," which has again no meaning without reference to sound, is to be found repeatedly mentioned in the Upanishads.

The figure of cloth or of something woven, as applied to Ethereal Space, and indeed to the whole universe, conceived as *yajña*, "sacrifice" (to be explained later), is also often met with in Vedic texts.

One of the alternative names for Ākāsha, Ethereal Space, is *vyoman*, which is derived from *ve* or *vā*, "weaving," with the prefix *vi*, "diversely," and thus means literally "webbing," the significance of which will now be understood. Because *vyoman*, Ethereal Space, is literally a webbing of lines, living though imaginary (*dishah*), like spreading-out (*ā*) reeds (*kāsha*), going everywhere and then turning back and coiling round like matted locks of hair which Shiva the Benign Lord wears, he is spoken of as *vyoma-kesha*, "space-haired." Slightly varying the figure, it is only the straightgoing aspects of the lines which are likened to his hair, while their curving and coiling aspects are spoken of as the divine life-giving stream of Gangā (the heavenly Ganges), meandering through the hair. Each of the straight lines is also symbolized as a "Linga" of which no limit can be found; neither Brahmā nor Vishnu—one going upward and another downward ceaselessly for ages—could ever come to the Linga's end. The coiling are in that case pictured as serpents twining round the Linga. One other symbolism is that of Gangā issuing from Vishnu's feet, or highest path (*parama pada*), as from a spring of honey (*madhu-utsa*). There are numerous other forms of symbolism representing this conception of Ākāsha as a webbing of straight and curved lines of living energy.

fire representing the universal Fire that burns on the altar of Ethereal Space—that Fire into whose secret Nachiketas was initiated by Yama and which the seers and Yogins behold in their inmost being as Tejas, Light of boundless, spaceless, timeless Life and Awareness.[44]

It may not be impossible that the fire burning in the bush, visioned of Moses, may have been this universal spiritual Fire burning in the midst of the bush of these rigid lines of Ākāsha—of firmament—radiating from the center of Being, who is again conceived in some forms of symbology as a mountain (*parvata*).[45]

This appearance of Ākāsha in the way mentioned above is described technically in some of the systems of philosophy by the statement: "From the variations produced in the Bhūtamātrā of Sound there comes into manifestation Ethereality, or Ether (*ākāsha*)."

This is said because there need be no other experience whatsoever for the realization of the varieties of Sound but that of all directions, or, which is the same thing, of an indefinite something going out in all directions. There may be other experiences, as indeed there will be at a later stage; but these need not be there or necessarily precede that of Ākāsha.

Next let us suppose that we are immersed in a sea of uniform temperature which has already ceased to be perceived as an object, and that there are as yet no other objects but the already produced varieties

---

[44] Characterized in an old stanza as *dikkālādyanavacchinnānantacinmātramūrti.*

[45] That the all-upholding *dishah,* spreading everywhere, are Lines of Force and weave themselves into the Ether or Ethereal Space need not be an absurd idea. The theories of physics tend to do away with the conception of the ether as a "jelly-like" substance. And science may find that there may still be the ether, but made up of lines of force, as the Vedic conception has it.

of Sound, as would be the case under the circumstances we are considering. Then let us further suppose that there arises a variety in this uniform and
homogeneous temperature and we begin to feel it to
be more hot or more cold, a freezing or a burning
sensation. What would be the necessary and inevit-
able experience accompanying or following this variation in the sensation of temperature? It would be,
says the Vedic tradition, the experience of "ticklish"
movements like a gentle aerial current. And it is this
experience which is technically Air (Vāyu). There
need not necessarily be any other experience whatsoever for the realization of variations in temperature, but that of this gentle air-like flow, although
there may be, as later there will be, other experiences
as well, accompanying that of variations in temperature. In other words, from the experience of variation in Temperature-in-general there arises the experience of Air, or, which is the same thing, there
is produced Air.

Speaking technically, from the variations produced
in the Bhūtamātrā of Temperature there comes into
manifestation Aeriality, or Air (vāyu).

Again let us suppose that we are face to face with
an all-enveloping mass of Color-in-general, which,
for reasons mentioned above, has already ceased to
form an object of experience, although there may be
present in the experience, at this stage, the already
produced perceptions of the varieties of Sound and
Temperature and consequent Ethereal Space and Air.
Then let us imagine that there suddenly arises the
experience of a variety of colors. What would be
the necessarily consequent experience when this is
realized? The obvious answer would perhaps be that
it is the experience of Form and Shape (rūpa). But
a little reflection will show that it would really be
the experience of a something, some power or energy,

which builds up, transforms, or destroys forms. For when there suddenly arises a patch of color in the vacancy of the horizon, it is no doubt seen as a shape or form of some sort, but this form may be said to be the same thing as the color, because without it, color, as thus perceived at the time, has hardly any meaning. And therefore the perception of colors of this type means really the same thing as the perception of forms; so much so that, instead of saying that there arose the experience of a variety of colors one might as well say that there arose the experience of a variety of forms.[46] The experience of form, therefore, cannot be called a consequent experience in the same way as Ethereal Space (*ākāsha*) is the consequent experience to that of a variation in Sound-in-general or the experience of Aeriality is consequent to that of variation in Temperature-in-general. The experience which is really a consequent one in this case is that of a something, some power, energy, or movement which produces, transforms, or destroys the forms. This form-producing energy or movement is technically called Fire (Agni), by which term, however, we must not understand—and this cannot be too strongly emphasized, in view of the numerous and gross misconceptions that have been formed of its meaning—anything but this energy or power of which the only function is combustion or chemical action (*jvalana* or *pāka*), which again means simply building up, producing or reproducing, and destroying shapes, bringing shapes and forms into existence from what is formless and changing one form into some other or others and *vice versa*.

It is thus from the experience of variety in Color-in-general that there arises the experience of Fire. Or, speaking technically, from the variations pro-

---

[46] The Sanskrit word *rūpa* means both color and form, as well as beauty.

duced in the Bhūtamātrā of Color there comes into manifestation Fire *(agni)*, the Form-builder.

Next let us imagine that our experience of Flavor-in-general, which has already ceased to be an object of perception, changes into that of a variety of flavors. The necessary experience consequent on this would be, as can easily be seen, that of movement, as of moisture, i.e. liquidity; for what is tasted, i.e. different flavors, is always found associated with the feeling of moisture, without any other sensation so necessarily accompanying it. It is this experience of moisture or liquidity thus produced which is technically and symbolically called Water (Ap). It is therefore stated: From the variations produced in the Bhūtamātrā of Flavor there comes into manifestation Water *(ap)*. This may appear strange, and even absurd, in view of the fact that, unlike the senses of sight, hearing, and temperature-feeling, the sense of taste plays such a small and unimportant part; it does not seem possible that, from this comparatively unimportant experience of tasting a variety of flavors, there can be produced so vast a result as the experience of liquidity, which forms so great a part of the physical world.

But we must not forget that, at the stage we are considering, there is as yet no physical body of the soul, and the senses are therefore not localized in the body. Therefore the sense of taste and that of smell are, like all the other senses, all over the soul, as it were. Moreover the Self, in these stages, feels himself to be but a nonspatial point *(anu)*, since the Self has now ceased to feel himself to be the infinitely great and since he cannot be anything of measurable dimensions, inasmuch as all measurable forms are perishable and the Self is not. These sensations of taste and smell are therefore at this stage as all-filling and overwhelming as any others.

There is thus nothing really absurd in the idea that Water, i.e. what is perceived as moist or liquid, is produced from the experience of variation in Flavor-in-general.

Finally let us suppose that our experience of Odor-in-general is, similarly and under similar circumstances, changed into that of a variety of odors. The necessary experience consequent on this would be not that of "all directions," nor of Air or Fire, nor even of anything liquid or watery, although all these may be, and indeed often are, present at the time. None of these needs, however, be present. The only experience which is absolutely necessary and is necessarily present is simply that of a something standing still, staying, or sticking, as it were, to the sense of smell, but felt at this stage all over the soul. It is, in other words, an experience of something stable, i.e. of stability, which is the essential characteristic of all things solid and hard, i.e. earthy, of the nature of Earth. We may therefore say that with the experience of variety in Odor-in-general there is also produced the experience of stability or solidity from which again come all such experiences as hardness, roughness, pressure or weight, and so on, i.e. all that is meant by the technical Earth (Prithivī) .[47]

Or, as it may be stated technically: From the variations produced in the Bhūtamātrā of Odor there comes into manifestation Earth, the Principle of Stability and Solidity, or, which is the same thing, the stable or solid thing (*prithivī*) .

Nor is there anything absurd in this statement; for, as may be repeated once more, the sensation of the varieties of smell, as experienced at this stage, is, as it were, all over the soul and is as all-filling and overwhelming as any others and the consequent experience as great and mighty.

---

[47] Cf. *yat kathinam sā prithivī* (Sharīraka Upanishad).

Thus from the experience of variation in the five general objects of perception there are produced also the five important factors of the Physical, namely Ethereal Space (Ākāsha) and the four others technically and symbolically called Air (Vāyu), Fire (Agni), Water (Ap), and Earth (Prithivī) —ingredients collectively designated in Sanskrit by the technical name of Bhūtas, i.e. the ever passing Have-been's (never the Are's), which are but Ghosts[48] of the Real, the one ever-abiding Being that is the inmost self of them all, as of the universe.

With the appearance of Earth (in the technical sense) as the principle of Solidity, we have reached the end of the process of Ātman's limiting and involving himself in various grades of subjective and objective existence.

The Bhūta Earth is thus only Ātman, the Self, who has become limited and involved to the uttermost degree and has ceased to move. It is the lowest and most restricted range of movements (*jagat*) of which the universe is made. In other words, Earth is only Ātman that has become a point and moves and waves within the greatest possible restriction and acts as the odor-stimulating element in the universal structure.

Similarly it is only Ātman who, having become so many points, appears as Water, Fire, and Air (all in the technical sense), moving and waving in ways and within ranges that are many and diverse.

Ethereal Ākāsha is, likewise, nothing but Ātman stretching himself out, without a conceivable end, as an infinite number of firm, rigid lines which are the directions of Space—have indeed woven themselves into the fabric of Ethereal Space (*bhūtākāsha*) —and are, at the same time, upholders of things in their various positional relations.

---

[48] The word *bhūta* means both "ghost" and "what has been."

Indeed, all the stages of Self-limitation on the part of Ātman are, as already said, so many entities, inasmuch as they are only Ātman involved in particular ways. And they all exist, as it were, simultaneously together from the Ultimate Being downward, or onward, to Earth.

Moreover, Ātman appears not as one particle only of Earth or one entity only in each of the stages. On the contrary, the moment there begins in a stage the operation of space and time, which will be considered presently, there is produced in that stage a multiplicity of forms. Ātman is inexhaustible and the process ceaseless. The one Ātman, therefore, appears, in every stage where there are space-time conditions, ceaselessly in countless forms. This the Ātman does in a manner which is somewhat like that of a single vital cell multiplying itself into countless numbers. These countless forms of Ātman in the different planes react one upon the other and are interrelated in an infinite variety of ways. There is therefore no solipsistic isolation in any of the stages where there is the experience of Space and Time. There is no loneliness even where, as in the Ultimate Being, Space and Time are not. For loneliness has meaning only where there is limitation and a feeling of want. In any case, in every stage and plane where there is a space-time frame, there is also an inexhaustible number of individual souls, as there is in the physical world an exhaustless number of physical particles, Paramānus, ions, electrons, or whatever else may be the ultimate physical constituents; from the Vedic point of view, each is a Soul, a form of Ātman, a Monad, but limited and restricted to the uttermost.

And if there is no solipsistic isolation in regard to the experiencing subject, neither is there one common universe of experience for all. That is to say, each experiencing subject has a universe which is absolutely and entirely his own.[49] If, therefore, we speak of our really different universes as one and the same—when, for instance, we say "I am seeing the same sun as you are"—that is only because what is experienced is assumed to be similar. The universe of John is the same as the universe of James in exactly the same sense as the picture seen by one eye of a man is the same as that seen by his other eye. It is a well-known fact that a person really sees two different pictures with his two eyes; but he thinks and speaks of them as one and the same picture because they are similar and, as a rule, coalesce with each other. Or, our different universes are one and the same in the sense that a particular play acted by one and the same dramatic company is one and the same play for different groups of people seeing it on different occasions. That this is so needs little argument, once we realize that each one of us really experiences what is primarily built up of his own individual sensations, thoughts, and ideas, even though these are induced in the individual, in spheres of time and space, by the operation on him of what appears as outside, such as wave lengths and other stimulating movements. The idea may, however, be further illustrated in the following manner. Suppose two persons see before them a rod which appears to each to be, say, five feet long. In reality, it is quite possible that one man sees it as a much longer rod than does the other man, the eyes of the former having, let us say, a sort of magnifying power which is not possessed by the other. And if the two men still speak of the rod as five feet long, it is because the foot-measure is seen proportionately elongated by the man with the magnifying eyes and the elongated measure is contained five times in the rod, exactly as the shorter measure, in the case of the second man,

[49] In technical language, universes, like the experiences of them, are *prātisvika*, "each one's own."

is contained the same number of times in the rod which the latter sees. Thus, while they may really see two different rods, they may yet speak of them as one and the same rod only because of the similarity, and even equality and constancy, of a certain relation subsisting between the rods experienced and the foot-measures, which, like the rods, are really different for the two different individuals. It is only in this sense of a certain similarity and constancy of relations that the universes experienced by different individuals are one and the same.

Thus it happens that if there is a multiplicity of experiencing entities as individuals, there is also a corresponding multiplicity of universes which are spoken of as the same by a sort of tacit convention.

This multiplicity of entities in the various stages is at once the cause and effect of what we experience as Space and Time. They begin to appear when multiplicity appears and Ātman as subject begins to experience an object, or a series of objects, which, however, are only himself in another phase and seen away in countless directions and in ceaseless succession; and it is this experience of direction and succession which is the essence of Space and Time.

But Space and Time are not the same in all the stages, so that near and far, now and then, simultaneity and succession, cannot have the same meaning everywhere and under all conditions. In other words, Space and Time are uniform and obey uniformly the same sets of laws in relation only to a particular stage, say, the physical, but are totally different when experienced in relation to a different stage, for instance, the psychical. There is thus no absolute Space and no absolute Time, experienced in one uniform manner in all the stages of existence. Thus it is said that Space and Time as experienced by a Deva (a superhuman being, to be explained presently) are different from Space and Time as experienced by man. All of us can form some idea of this relativity of Space and Time from our common experiences in dreams as compared with experiences in the waking state. A man may be having dreams which would give him the idea of ranging over wide distances in space and of stretching across long years of time. But while thus dreaming he may not have slept for more than five minutes of time as experienced in waking life and while he has not moved away even an inch of space as measured physically. But suppose he never woke up, and yet we had some means of knowing his experiences and comparing them with the experiences of a man who was, let us further suppose, keeping watch over him and was awake in physical space and time. Would we not then say that what are only the limited space of the room and five minutes of physical time to the waking man are, as it were, wide distances and long years to the sleeping person? We have to use the qualifying expression "as it were," because there can be no real comparison between the two sets of Space-Time experiences, the two Space-Time frames, which are really on two entirely different planes. Still this would give us some idea of how Space-Time frames differ in different stages, so that one particular frame is true and uniform in relation only to a particular stage, plane, or set of experiences,[50] but not so when applied to a different plane.

---

[50] This ancient idea of the relativity of space and time based on experience and justifiable purely on psychological grounds may be compared with Einstein's Theory of Relativity based on mathematical reasoning.

PART II

The universe produced from the one undivided Ātman by the on-rolling process of manifestation (*vivarta*) is thus a unified system, a mighty organism in which the inmost nucleus and pervading Spirit and Self is the one abiding Being, the one Supreme Person (Purusha) in his aspect as Brahman, the Word, as Īsha, the Lord, who ordains that every moving thing—and all things are moving—in this ever-moving universe shall yet move and dwell within ranges which are inexorably fixed and can be transgressed only at the risk of self-destruction as an individual entity, even though the ranges and limits can be so widened as to be coextensive with the whole universe—can even be entirely transcended by following a path of living, behavior, and action that is in harmony with the All, with the universal movement, with the Self and Spirit of the All.

In this mighty living organism that is the Universe there is nothing really dead or absolutely unconscious. On the contrary, like every cell in a living, healthy body, every part and every thing in the universe is alive, though many parts are, as it were, in a comatose state; every part, every particle in it is ensouled, inspirited, by the All-aware, All-feeling Being that is Ātman. What appears as dead and unconscious, yet has the universal life and awareness in it as its inmost core, but completely cabined, cribbed, and confined—buried deep and as if in sound, dreamless sleep.

There is thus the Being of life, feeling and awareness, even in the most unfeeling stone, as in every
single ion, in each electron, Anu and Paramānu.
And he is there not in part, as a fragment, but in
his full, unidivided being: there can be no division
in the Being, no real limitation to him in Space,
Time, or any other way.

This is beautifully illustrated in the story of Prahlāda, even though that is found outside of the Vedas.
We are told how, in order to rescue Prahlāda from
the heartless tortures inflicted by his wicked father,
the Being Divine, in response to Prahlāda's burning
love for him, appears in all his glory from out a
crystal pillar in which he, in all his fullness, has remained hidden, deeply buried, as the inmost core of
every particle in that cold dead structure.

This is why the Hindu maintains that the Vedic
seers were telling nothing but simple unvarnished
truth when they declared that they perceived life and
awareness in and behind every part and phenomenon
of nature, visible and invisible, and called each manifestation a Deva, a divine flashing-forth from the one
Central Being. The Devas, crudely and incorrectly
interpreted as "gods," but more properly "angels,"[51]
are thus no personifications of nature and its phenomena, but the very spirit and Self of the Universe
seen through Nature's forms as through a prism. Indeed, it is to this day held in India that Nature and
her phenomena, being but aspects of the one all-
aware Being, can be consciously and feelingly com-
muned with even now; and that the experiences of
the ancient Rishi (Seer) can even today be, and indeed are, repeated by those duly qualified for the task.
As a matter of fact, the Vedic worship performed even
now, and three times a day, by Brahmans and others

---

[51] Probably identical etymologically with *angiras*, which is often
used as an epithet of Devas.

is a still living expression of this truth; so that when a Brahman offers his chant of ancient Vedic Words (Mantras) to the Sun or the Waters, he knows he is addressing himself really to the Spirit, to those aspects of the Being that are behind these physical forms of Nature, whether singly and collectively, whether as separate cells and monads or as different groups of them constituting diverse organic wholes.[52] He knows, too, that he certainly is not worshiping phenomena that are really dead and are only personified in his imagination.

Indeed, from the Vedic point of view, Nature and the universe, visible or invisible, is much more than a living organism. It is a mighty hierarchy of living beings, superhuman, human, and subhuman. The subhuman is as obvious as the human, whereas the superhuman comprises, among others, Devas and human souls that have attained ranges of awareness and movement surpassing those of ordinary man.

At the head of this hierarchy stands he who represents the first step taken by the Being starting on the path of self-limitation; he is Brahman, the Word, or, as he is also named, Īsha, Īshvara, the Lord.

From another point of view he is the last product of the Universal Process (*vivarta*), being the final stage in the path backward, as it were homeward, to the Ultimate Being. For, once Ātman has reached the stage of utmost limitation as in Earth (technical), he begins to retrace his steps with a view to going back, ultimately, to the state of abiding Being in his undimmed glory. The result is the gradual unfolding of Life and beings—living, conscious, selfconscious, and even superconscious, transcending the self of the

---

[52] Thus from the Vedic point of view there is more truth in what is despisingly called "animism" than in the theory of an unfeeling and unintelligent Nature, i.e. the theory of materialism advanced by scientists and their followers in the last century, though discarded now by at least a number of distinguished men of science.

ego. In other words, the fruits of the endeavor to reach back to the Supreme Divine state of Being are life germinal, vegetable life, and then gradually man, superman, and the angelic hosts, stretching onward toward Brahman, who is thus, in this sense, the ultimate product of the process—a process of which only the second, the returning half, may be said to correspond, but partly, to what is now known as Evolution, especially Emergent Evolution, which, as a process, undoubtedly means the unfolding of what already exists as something involved in previous stages, out of which it comes, so that its actual appearance is only an emerging.

The universe, as thus conceived, consists not only of beings that are living and intelligent, actually or potentially, but also of certain Grades, Planes, or Fields of Vision (*loka*), as they are called, i.e. worlds. These Planes are counted as either three or seven, according as the last (or first) five are counted separately or taken together as one.

When counted as three the Planes (Lokas) are:

1. The Physical, or the Earth, corresponding to the physical body of man (Bhūr and Prithivī) ;
2. The Psychical, corresponding to what has been defined as the soul of man, namely life (Prāna), Concrete Mentality (Manas) including all the sense powers, and Ego (Ahamkāra or Vijñāna), behaving together as a unit (Bhuvas or Antariksha) ;
3. The Spiritual, corresponding to the Mahat in man (Svar or Suvar, the Heavenly World) [53].

---

[53] Cf. the oft-repeated expression *svarge loke mahīyate,* and note the play on *mahīyate,* the suggestion of Mahat. In the sevenfold division, Svar is what corresponds to ego taken by itself, and the next Loka, Mahas, is the one corresponding to Mahat. The Lokas transcending Mahas in the sevenfold counting are Jana, Tapas, and Satya. They correspond to states of experience which, it is maintained, can be had only by yoga. They are not easily distinguishable intellectually and hence are generally not mentioned in theoretical studies. In the Trika Philosophy, however, their

They are also counted as five, corresponding to what are called the "sheaths" or coverings (*kosha*) of Ātman, the sheaths themselves being only the body and the other factors in man regarded from a particular point of view. These Koshas or sheaths are:

1. The Physical (in this connection called Anna, "Food")
2. The Vital (Prāna)
3. The Mental (Concrete Mentality, Manas)
4. The Ego (called Vijñāna in this connection)
5. The Spirit, i.e. Mahat-Ātman and Asat or Avyakta (in this connection called Ānanda)

As the Koshas are five, the Lokas or planes related to them are, from this point of view, also the same number.

All this is produced by Purusha, the Supreme Person, who, as Ātman, binds and sacrifices himself ceaselessly on the "cross of well-being" (*svastika*), pouring out his "life-blood" in unending streams of good will and love to the "four quarters" of space.[54] His is a sacrifice of joy, brought about by love (*ānanda*), which of itself knows no bounds. To vary an ancient metaphor, forth from Purusha, in the act of ceaseless sacrifice, does the universe stream, an unceasing spring of joy that is ever at play on the space-time green in far-spreading, never-ending sprays.[55]

---

subjective correspondences are well recognized in the Tattvas transcending what is called "Purusha," which name is given in that system to a conditioned aspect of the ultimate Being. All these lokas are daily meditated on in the Vedic worship as it is now practiced in the form of Samdhyā by means of the famous Gāyatrī. They are then regarded as only the objective effulgence (*bhargas*) of the ultimate Being conceived as Savitri, who is at the same time sought to be realized subjectively as our inmost self, stimulating all thoughts within us.

[54] The meaning of the cross and sacrifice by crucifixion, and of the crucifixion of Christ, as conceived by Yogins, will be discussed in a subsequent essay.

[55] Cf. *sphuranti shīkarā yasmād ānandasyāmbare 'vanau*, "from whom are blossoming forth sprays of love and joy in heaven and earth" (Yogavāsishtha).

To use still another figure, the universe is a feast of love and joy in which Brahman himself is both the "food" and its "eater," both what is enjoyed and the enjoyer (the object and the subject). But as if the more to enjoy the food, to have the joy of eating it by countless mouths, Brahman spreads himself out in multifarious forms, so that each such form of him is a new mouth, a new aspect, with which to eat the food. Viewed in another way, this feast of love and joy spread by Brahman is enjoyed all the more by him when he shares it with all his creatures, even though they are but himself in diverse garbs.

And Ātman has the joyous feast, and shares the enjoyment with all the beings that are the universal hierarchy, not once but countless times, from all eternity without a beginning. For, as already said, he goes on alternating, from beginningless time, between the two phases of Manifestation (*shrishti,* throwing out) and Absorption (*pralaya,* dissolution), so that, though there is the beginning of a particular universe, there is no absolute first start to the series of universes, which are all linked together as cause and effect.

It thus happens that at no time in the history of a universe are beings, constituting it, exclusively of the lowest type, or absolute savages. On the contrary, the first products in a new universe are beings of the loftiest character and widest possible range of experience. For when a universe passes away into dissolution, the results accomplished therein, the various beings produced at its different stages, are not completely lost. There is absolutely no loss or waste of labor here, no energy destroyed. Rather all beings, as it were, fall asleep at their respective stations as Brahman falls asleep at his. And on a new universe coming into manifestation, they all, as it were, wake up just when in the universal process that particular stage is again reached at which, in the previous universe, they had fallen asleep; and there each being, as it were, merely resumes his march of life at the exact point where a halt had been called. And as it is the higher stages, i.e. the stages which are, as it were, nearest to Purusha, that reappear at the beginning and in the earlier life of the universe, the beings who wake up first are just those who had attained the greatest self-unfoldment in the past. And they are the Sages, Seers, Rishis, and Prophets who bring over wisdom from across the gulf of ages and become teachers and guides, masters and kings, of those that are inferior to them in power and evolution, whether as products of a past universe or of the new one. This is the reason why it is the universal tradition of all ancient peoples and civilizations that gods walked among men in the earlier days and that their first teachers and the founders of the arts and civilization were beings of a much higher order than themselves, were heroes, gods, and demigods, patesis and prophets, seers (Rishis), perfected beings (Siddhas), and fathers (Pitris).

This is also the reason why we find such lofty thoughts and ideas, unexcelled royal and imperial power, pomp, and glory, and such mighty lawgivers at the beginning of a racial development. And that is why, incidentally, the Vedas are not the babblings of an infant race, but contain wonderful wisdom, if properly understood. Of course, this does not mean that the whole Vedic literature in every part and detail is of the loftiest character. Besides being compilations of a mixed character, perhaps from the start, the Vedic texts are thousands of years old—the oldest literary records of Indian culture. As such they certainly have not come down to us absolutely unchanged or unmixed further with inferior material of later ages, even though the received texts have been preserved for at least three thousand years without undergoing any serious alterations. Nevertheless the fundamental ideas of the Vedas are of the loftiest character.

Even in parts supposed to be inferior and polytheistic (the latter perhaps the most absurd charge possible),[56] the Vedas are a way of describing nature and the universe viewed as a living organism, of which every part, every limb, even every cell, being but the one all-aware Ātman veiled in various ways and degrees, can think, feel, and, as it were, talk; in much the same way as, in the opposite direction, science is a description of Nature and her workings, but looked upon as only mechanical movements of something dead and unintelligent. The Vedas are, in other words, the Science of Nature and the Universe conceived as an organic whole, as a living hierarchy—a science (*veda*) framed by superior beings from a past universe.

In any case this is a view of things which need not be lightly set aside, especially as the other view, namely, of an unintelligent origin of things, cannot possibly be regarded as a definitely established fact. If, under the circumstances, the doctrine of an intelligent origin of the universe, as advocated by all schools of Vedic philosophy and most ancient schools of other peoples and practically all religions[57] is ac-

---

[56] The Vedas are no more polytheistic than they are, to coin a new word, "polyanthropoistic." The so-called gods of the Vedas have no more independent and separate existences than men have: both men and gods are equally so many different manifestations of the only reality, Brahman, who is the one God, if God he must be called. It is so absurd to call the Vedas polytheistic that Max Müller was obliged to coin a new term "henotheism" for the Vedic conception of the Devas.

[57] The doctrines of an intelligent origin of things are chiefly of two types. One of these is represented by the religions of Semitic origin which believe in a god like a mighty king, like a "Caesar," as Prof. A. N. Whitehead has it. This god, according to such religions, is the creator of everything. But he, too, can create, even at the beginning of the universe, the highest types of beings.

cepted as truth, then there is no reason to doubt that the beings appearing at the earliest stages of the universe are higher types developed in a past one. Indeed there may come a time when this view of the origin of things will be fully accepted as the only rational one; and when or if this is done the philosophy of history as well as the whole of the early history of civilization will have to be rewritten. In this new view, or rather the oldest view merely restated anew, progress will, of course, be recognized; but it will be progress like that in the education of a boy who has grown up into manhood. It is true, the boy has made progress in knowledge and experience; but it is also true that he has done so with the aid and co-operation of his teachers and elders who were already more advanced than he; and it would not be a correct account of his educational progress if the part that his teachers and elders played in it were left out. To give a complete history of the educational progress of the boy we must take note also of the help of the teachers. In the same way, if the Vedic point of view in regard to the origin of things be accepted, then we have also to admit that, in the progress of the universe and individuals therein, there has been no time when higher types of beings were not present helping and guiding the growth and development of types lower than themselves.

It is, however, not necessary that these higher types of beings, especially at the beginning, should always exist in the physical world. As a matter of fact such early teachers and guides and founders of civilization have often been regarded as superphysical entities.

As a matter of fact, it is the belief of such religions that he does so. The second type of doctrine of the intelligent origin of the universe is what we have explained above as the Vedic view. Substantially this is the view also of Buddhism and Jainism, both of which, along with Brahmanism, hold that the present universe is only one in a beginningless series, reappearing and disappearing from time to time.

And it has been believed that even as superphysical entities they have inspired human beings who have caught their ideas often as flashes of inspiration without knowing the sources from which they came.[58]

How the past is revived and the beings of a past universe wake up in a new one, and in what manner many of them do so with a full and detailed memory of the past, are topics which have been treated in many a text. One illustration of the process is to be found in the story of Vāmadeva, who, it is recorded, began singing the song of his past memory immediately on waking up, and proclaimed: "I once was Manu and again the Spirit of the Sun."[59] That beings can thus reappear from a past universe should not be difficult of comprehension for those who believe that they themselves will continue to exist as individual entities after death. For if they can thus endure as individuals in a bodiless condition, why cannot this

---

[58] It was the daily practice of the Buddha, we are told in the Pāli books, to wake up, like all spiritual men in India, in that early hour before the dawn known as *brāhmamuhūrta*, when, in the beautiful words of J. S. Hoyland, quoted by Prof. Eddington (*Science and the Unseen World*, pp. 44-55) the veil between the seen and the unseen seems to be thinnest. He would then survey the world with his "divine Buddha eye" and pick out those who were ready for spiritual guidance and then send out to them his thoughts, which would be received by the persons so selected often as inspirations, but coming as though from within themselves. It is in this way, the followers of the Vedas hold, that we are often inspired by unseen entities; some of them may have physical existences but at a distance or out of sight, while others are entirely superphysical.

[59] This occurs first in Rig-Veda 4.26 and is quoted in Brih. Up. 1.4.10. In the latter passage it is explained by certain commentators as referring to the recovery of the past memory by Vāmadeva on the realization of Brahman. But the section is one dealing with the origin of things at the beginning of a new world-period and it is therefore more logical to take the Rig-Vedic mantra quoted therein as illustrating the recollection, in a new universe, of the memory of things in a previous one. The passage in the Upanishad really means: "Whoever of the Devas woke up (at the beginning of a *kalpa*) he became the same as he was before, and that was the case with whoever woke up of the Rishis and of men." This means that these also, like the Devas (angels), again occupy their respective stations, similar to those in a previous universe.

be done by other beings, especially those who have attained states of development higher than those of average humanity, i.e. have grown stronger in character and reached wider ranges of experience? And the rationality and probable truth of the idea should be still less difficult of comprehension for those who accept reincarnation as a fact. For this reappearance of beings from a past universe is only a different application of the same principle that governs the rebirth of souls in this present universe of our own.

And as a new birth of a soul in the present universe is governed by the law of cause and effect—the law of Karma, as it is called—i.e. the law of justice, of a perfect and absolute adjustment of things, so is the appearance of a new universe from a past one governed by the same moral law. In other words, the repeated appearance and disappearance of universes is governed by a law of absolute adjustment, of moral justice (*dharma*), which is thus the foundation on which the universe is built up.[60]

And the result which is aimed at by all this ceaseless activity and movement, this repeated appearance and disappearance of the universe, is the production of perfected beings, perfected in every respect, so that each of the final products shall be fully and completely divine and independent—all-knowing and all-powerful, each Brahman-like, each Brahman himself. But this final result is reached and an individual finally realizes the ultimate end, once and for all, only after long ages of countless births and deaths, not only in this physical world but also in other states of existence (*loka*).[61] The process is thus very slow indeed. It can, however, be accelerated by the method of self-training and self-realization known

---

[60] On this subject see the writer's *Hindu Realism*.
[61] For a fuller exposition of the doctrine of reincarnation consult the writer's *Hindu Realism*.

as yoga.[62]

The earliest mention of yoga by name in the Vedic texts occurs in the Katha and Shvetāsvatara Upanishads. Practically all the fundamental ideas of yoga, even as found in the later systematized and most authoritative treatise on the subject (the Yoga-sūtras of Patañjali) are to be found—at least in a germinal form—in these two Upanishads, which both date back to a remote antiquity. It is, however, not necessary here to go into a detailed exposition of these texts on yoga. Only the main principles underlying the art need be set forth here; these are only a few and comparatively simple. They may be stated as follows.

The source of all knowledge and experience is really within our own inmost Self, who is also the ultimate Being.

Even in the most external of the states of experience, namely the physical, the only things which may be said to be outside are the stimulating movements, wave lengths. But these, too, are outside only under conditions of Space and Time as governing the physical, and, to a certain extent, the psychical spheres of experience. The moment, however, we touch in conscious experience the state of Universal Ideation (Mahat) , i.e. what has been called by some the Spirit, and thereby pass into a condition where Space and Time have a totally different significance—where they do not exist as dividing agents—that very moment even the stimulating movements, the wave lengths, cease to be felt as anything external. Rather the sources of all such movements and waves are then discovered within—in oneself.

It thus happens that all knowledge, indeed all the universe, the whole "Kingdom of Heaven," is literally within us; it is within us as eternal, timeless, space-

---

[62] Etymologically the same word as "yoke," meaning "yoking" or "harnassing," i.e. disciplining oneself.

less, idealized objectivity lying in front of Ātman, the eternal Subject and untiring Enjoyer.

For, though the Self within is felt to be smaller than the small (*anor anīyān*), he is, on the other hand, greater than the great (*mahato mahīyan*) [63]— greater than the earth, greater than the heaven, greater than the region between, greater than all the worlds. All active endeavor is he, the Ātman, all-desire, all-odor, all-taste is he; he is the fulfillment of all this. He is within the inmost heart of man.[64]

Within the heart is therefore "Ethereal Space far extending as Ether and Space without. Within this, in truth, lie hidden both heaven and earth, both Fire and Air, both Sun and Moon, the lightning and the stars. Whatever else here in the external is and whatever is not—all that is hidden in this, in the heart."[65] All we need to do, therefore, is to tap this course of knowledge and experience within.

These are ideas which are not peculiar to the Vedas or to India; they have been experienced and uttered likewise by many in the Occident. Robert Browning, for instance, a poet belonging to a nation supposed to be the most matter-of-fact and practical, has expressed the thought in *Paracelsus* in the following vivid passage:

> Truth is within ourselves; it takes no rise
> From outward things, whate'er you may believe.
> There is an inmost center in us all,
> Where truth abides in fullness; and around,

---

[63] Katha Upanishad 2.20.
[64] See Chāndogya Upanishad 3.14.2-4.
[65] Chāndogya Upanishad 8.1.3. The meaning of all things existing together in a timeless state is not that this is a mere collection of things as we know them through the physical senses in physical space and time. They exist as a general and universal synthesis; this is very different from a mere aggregate, from which the synthetic ideal state differs as much as an ideal triangle, i.e. triangularity, differs from a mere aggregate of triangles of various shapes and dimensions.

Wall upon wall, the gross flesh hems it in,
This perfect, clear perception—which is truth.
A baffling and perverting carnal mesh
Binds it, and makes all error: and to KNOW
Rather consists in opening out a way
Whence the imprisoned splendour may escape,
Than in effecting entry for a light
Supposed to be without.

But if the whole Kingdom of Heaven is within and if all knowledge and all science are lying buried in our inmost self, how is it, then, that we do not always realize these in experience?

The obstacles in our way are only two, though caused in various ways, namely dullness and distraction (*āvarana* and *vikshepa*). Whenever a person endeavors, without full training and right preparation, to be silent and listen to the movement of the higher states of being within himself, to the Song Divine within, he either falls asleep, which is the effect of dullness, or his mind is distracted and wanders, as it were, all over the universe. But if he can hold his consciousness in a tense state, keenly intent upon what is going on within the uttermost depth of his being, without either falling asleep or letting the mind wander, he will gradually but surely begin to be responsive to the subtlest throb, the most gentle whisper of his Spirit, of the Self within. With constant practice, the whisper will grow into such loud tones and will swell into such volume that it will drown the whole universe.

The principle may be illustrated in the following manner. Let us suppose that there are strains of music coming to a man from some distance, being borne on the wind, and just audible at first as a faint note. Let us suppose further that our man concentrates his mind keenly and unwaveringly on that note, pouring out, as it were, his whole soul into the ear. It will be found that, as a result of this, the music that was at first heard as a very faint note has grown louder and louder till it has not only absorbed the man's entire attention and being, but has, as it were, filled the whole universe. Or, take the classic instance of that master of archery, Arjuna, the Pāndava prince, when, under the order of his teacher, he took aim at the eye of a bird sitting on a tree at a distance, and concentrated his soul on it. On being asked by the teacher what he was seeing at the time, Arjuna replied that he saw only the eye of the bird as filling the whole universe, and nothing else.

In some such way, by concentrating one's whole mind, soul, and consciousness on the Self within, one can be so fully conscious of him as to exclude all other movements of thought or feeling. But concentration of this character is impossible unless all dullness is entirely overcome and the mind and heart are freed from every distraction. The first step, therefore, is to be intensely active, so that idleness and laziness are entirely banished from life.

In the earlier stages of the soul's growth, when a man is still undeveloped in character and strong individuality is lacking, he can maintain such an active life only, or at least chiefly, when prompted by selfish interests which are felt, at the time, as other than or opposed to the interests of his fellow men. During these stages the code of moral behavior is what, in the Vedic view, is called "action with a personal desire" (sakāma karma). And the Vedas deliberately provide such a code in those parts of them which are technically known as karma kānda. When in these desireful stages of growth (sakāma), a man or nation would pray, for instance, that his or his nation's enemies may be killed, that victory may be gained by his side. For such men the Vedas have prescribed the

worship of and prayers to the Devas (angels, misinter-
preted as gods), who are superhuman entities and
have power to be of service to men. The Vedas would
regard it as an unspeakable blasphemy and sacrilege
that selfish prayers of the character referred to should
be addressed to the Ultimate Being or even to Brahman, the Word, who is not only the same and impar-
tial to all, but is equally the core of every existence.
For men of lower types, therefore, the Vedas have
deliberately enacted selfish codes of conduct which
are the only means to stimulate such men to activity
and thus enable them to overcome dullness. When,
however, souls of this type, after millions of years of
growth and countless embodiments, repeated births
and deaths—innumerable reincarnations, in short—
have gradually and laboriously developed a strong
character and individuality, they soon discover that
the very selfishness which has carried them so far and
which until then was very necessary is now proving
a great hindrance to further progress back to the
divine home in the Ultimate Being whence they have
strayed. For it is then seen how selfishness is the
most potent and prolific cause of all passion and all
disturbances of the mind, of distraction, the second
great obstacle in the path of yoga. When a soul has
reached this stage of growth, then only is it ready for
yoga proper, all previous endeavors and activities being but a prelude to it. This stage reached, a man
must find a way of still remaining intensely active—
in order to be free from dullness—and must at the
same time eliminate all causes of distraction, i.e.
eliminate from his heart and mind all selfish notions
and all thought of personal interests as separate from
and opposed to the interests of others, who are really
not others, but only himself in different forms. In
other words, he must change not so much his outward life, as his entire attitude both toward what

he may be doing and in his relations to the rest
of the universe. He should and must adopt such
an attitude as would enable him to engage in all
necessary and useful activities without a selfish mo-
tive and without being so involved in the doings
as not to be able to shake off their thoughts whenever it is desired to do so. This art of doing things
effectively and efficiently but without selfish mo-
tives and interests (technically "desire for fruit")
and without being helplessly involved in them
(technically "entanglement," *sanga*), is called Karma Yoga (Yoga of Action), and can be accomplished
in various ways. But the general principle is that,
negatively, the aspirant to the highest spiritual experience should refrain from thinking any thoughts,
having any feelings and emotions, or doing any
deeds which are likely to strengthen selfishness, i.e.
the sense of separation; and that, positively, he should
cultivate only such thoughts and feelings and practice only such deeds as will eliminate from his heart
all selfishness and foster in it an abiding attitude
and feeling of unity with every living thing and
being—and all things are living. This is needed,
moreover, because the realization in experience of
the Being within and all that it implies is at the
same time the realization in feeling of an absolute
oneness with the whole universe and everything in
it. Anything, therefore, which strengthens the feeling of separation (*bheda-buddhi*) from others, as
selfishness does, is the most serious obstacle to the
realization of the end sought by yoga.

In other words, the most essential foundation for
yoga is *active moral* life of the very highest order
possible. That is why Patañjali, the most authoritative expounder of the subject, mentions first moral
discipline of the strictest and highest character, under the technical names of Yama and Niyama, and

then lays down that the virtues to be cultivated by Yama and Niyama are the absolutely indispensable prerequisite for yoga. It is only after this that Patañjali speaks of the other steps of yoga. As a matter of fact, it is simply childish to talk of yoga unless the essential prerequisite in the shape of the highest moral life is first practiced and very largely developed. Then only can one really walk the path of yoga. The Upanishads are also most explicit on this point.[66] One of them (Ishā) insists that a man must never neglect his duties, which shall be done diligently, that he must not transgress the limits within which alone he can legitimately and fruitfully labor, and that he must rid himself of all greed and selfishness. Another proclaims that none who has not refrained completely from evil behavior and has not the peace of heart and head—has not learned

---

[66] It is surprising and incomprehensible that some people should prattle about the Vedic attitude as less ethical than certain others. The race and literature which could produce a Vājashravasa who made his son over to Death because of a word given casually; a Harishchandra who gave away a whole kingdom and would make a gift of his own body because of a promise to give away everything, though the promise was made on a misunderstanding; a Bhīshma who would not swerve even by an inch from his determined course in carrying out a given troth even when he had every opportunity and every temptation to do so and who remained a bachelor and only a king-maker instead of a king, which he could easily have been so many times; a Yudhishthira who was made to see Hell because he only slightly prevaricated and swerved from the truth and even that only when the Divine himself tempted him to do so (he would be no great character if he yielded to the temptation at the instigation of any lesser being); a Rāmachandra who put away his dearly beloved consort in order to carry out his kingly duties as he conceived them (perhaps mistakenly, as some would say) and would not take another in her place even required to do so for purposes of religious rites, but had a golden image of the Queen made to serve the religious need; a Sītā and a Sāvitrī, noblest examples of female chastity and devotion—a race and literature that could produce these and many similar characters and have not ceased doing so even now, knew and know the value of moral life and ethics far better than do most of their critics. One feels almost tempted to hurl back at such critics the cutting words of Kālidāsa: *parātisamdhānam adhīyate yair vidyeti e santu kilāptavācah* (Shakuntalā 5.25).

to hold his entire being absolutely tranquil (*samā-hita*) —can realize the ultimate Truth (Katha 2.24). The same Upanishad declares that he alone can attain the highest goal who has all his senses under perfect control and is ever alert in mind and ever pure in heart (Katha 3.8). In other words, the aspirant to yoga must at once be active, alert in mind, and absolutely tranquil in his heart and must cultivate the feeling of love and oneness with all. This is the first step.

Then there are conditions of the body which often greatly disturb the mind. The body therefore should be taken hold of as the second serious step—second not in sequence but as a matter of classification, so that it is to be followed, not after the first, but simultaneously with the cultivation of the highest possible moral virtue and character. This is done by following certain physical and physiological practices of a very specific character, a regimen which undoubtedly gives a person, as one sees daily illustrated, not only a complete mastery over the nervous and muscular systems of the body, but enables him to keep it in a perfect state of health.[67]

Next there is a third group of practices which are purely mental, leading up to what is called Samādhi, which is, in its ultimate form, the state of awareness of the Ātman himself as he is in his

---

[67] There are Yogins who maintain that—following the same principle as underlies the qualifying clause "if it be possible" in the prayer of Jesus for the taking away from him of the "cup" of crucifixion—all things may be possible, but it is not always right, or in Christian phraseology, is not in accordance with the "will of God," to do all things or get all things done. In the phraseology of the philosophy based on the Vedic view, man should not run away from Prārabdha Karma (to be explained later), but must face it. And it is on this principle that Yogins often allow themselves to suffer bodily torture, whether from disease or in other ways, even when they could easily prevent it. And they do this, it is held, not only on their own account—to meet their own Prārabdha—but also vicariously for others.

own true being,[68] absolutely free from and independent of all relations to any objectivity, which has
vanished away. This is also the Nirvāna of the
Buddha, the unlimited Awareness (anantam vijñānam) without any relation to Earth and Water, Fire
and Air, i.e. all objectivity, which has vanished from
its view (see Kevaddha Sutta, end). Nirvāna is described in exactly the same terms as applied to Brah-
man-Ātman in the Vedas, such as unborn, uncompounded, eternal, and the like.

This is the final goal; when this is realized, everything else is heard and seen, everything enjoyed,
life fulfilled to the uttermost.

This is the final answer to the question which,
thousands of years ago, Shaunaka asked of Angiras,
saying: "On what being by experience known, O
master, is all this [i.e. the universe] experienced
and known?"[69]

And this goal can be realized by a man gradually,
through various stages and only when he is perfect
in yoga; and this again is possible only when what
he appropriates from the universe, as physical, mental, and spiritual food, is so appropriated that the
act can serve only to purify his entire being as an
individual, by establishing the most complete, the
most perfect harmony between himself and the All.
When his being is thus purified, there arises before
him the firm, imperishable memory of his past existences, his countless births and deaths during millions of years covering many a world-period of Manifestation and Dissolution (shrishti and pralaya)
during which he has lived as an individual—imperishable memory because nothing, not even a jot or

---

[68] Cf. tadā drashtuh svarūpe avasthānam, Yogasūtra 1.3 Cf. Brih.
Up. 2.4.14, where Yājñavalkya describes Ātman, called there
Vijñātri, in his true and absolute state, in which there is no objectivity whatsoever.
[69] Mundaka Up. 1.1.3 (Cf. also Chāndogya Up. 6.1.2-3).

tittle of our experience is lost, but the fruits of all remain deeply buried in the unconscious strata of our being and now rise up before the perfected individual in full recollection.[70]

When this is accomplished, then only can the fetter of individuality—the illusory ego, forged with the links of experiences stretching far and away into the remotest past (only now remembered as a single whole)—be broken forever and the aspect of Ātman so long kept chained by that particular individuality set completely free.[71]

Ātman, thus set free from all limiting individuality and all relations to qualifying objectivity, is then one with the Ultimate Being; or, more accurately, he has now the realization, in awareness and feeling, of the oneness which, though existing always, has hitherto remained, as it were, quite forgotten and unnoticed. The perfect realization on the part of a person of this oneness of his inmost and utmost Self with the Ultimate Being is the experience of what is called objectless Samādhi, that state of awareness, mentioned above, from before which all objects have entirely vanished (*nirvikalpa-samādhi*).

But when he, as it were, descends from this state of transcendent objectless experience—that is, the state of supreme ecstatic vision—or, as it is also said, though incorrectly, he "wakes up" to a consciousness of objects as things outside, he enjoys and experiences everything, all objectivity, the whole universe in the same way as Brahman does.[72]

In other words, when he "wakes up" to objective

---

[70] Buddha is reported to have recovered the memories of eighty-four past world-periods, an immense stretch of time almost impossible of comprehension.

[71] Cf. Chāndogya Up. 7.26.2: *āhāra-shuddhau sattva-shuddhih; sattva-shuddhau dhruvā smritih; smriti-lambhe sarva-granthinām vipramokshah.*

[72] Cf. Taittirīya Up. 2.1; *so 'shnute sarvān kāmān saha brahmanā.*

life again from objectless experience, the universe changes its aspect completely. It is an experience which is comparable, though in a very faint manner, to the experience of change which the world undergoes in the eyes of one who is truly, "madly," in love. The idea may perhaps be made a little clearer in another way. Suppose the findings of physics in regard to the ultimate nature of matter are true, representing actual, objective facts. Suppose, in other words, that a physical object, say a table, is actually composed of ions and electrons, moving round nuclei, with interspaces between. Suppose, further, that a person has developed his power of vision to such an extent that his eye is able to magnify things immeasurably and see the ions and electrons composing the table. Now it is obvious that such a person, looking at the table, will no longer see what he saw before, or what others may be seeing now. On the contrary, instead of seeing the table of familiar experience, he would perceive now the "second" table of Prof. Eddington, consisting only of wave lengths and the like. In other words, what he would actually be seeing now would not be a table at all, but a whirling mass of ions and electrons. The table of familiar experience has for him vanished, and in its place he sees only a mass of points executing all kinds of beautiful movements.

In some such way the universe of his previous experience vanishes away from before the man who has realized Samādhi; what he experiences as the universe when he "wakes up" from Samādhi is a very different thing, is only the "vibrating thought" of Brahman as life pulsating through all Space and Time; and he feels himself to be one with that life and therefore with the whole universe as now seen.

Being one with all, he knows and experiences all; nothing is beyond his reach, nothing can remain hidden from his gaze; he has become all-knowing at will. "In himself he now sees all things and beings, equally as he sees himself in all things and beings."

For him life's uttermost purpose is fulfilled. Whatever wish or desire he now has, he finds satisfied at once: only he has no personal desires now, no interests which are opposed to the interests of the whole; such desires and such interests he has left behind long before he has reached the spiritual heights where he now habitually dwells.

The result is that righteousness is now a habit with him, no longer a virtue inasmuch as it is no longer an effort, a striving. Virtue is now his native nature: hitherto covered up with ignorance (*avid-yā*), with the illusory notion and feeling of a separate ego, an individual I, this natural state now shines out in its native glory and he cannot but be righteous, any more than fire can be anything but hot and burning. Hence he has now transcended all such conceptions as vice and virtue, which have meaning only insofar as we have an "evil nature," or rather, evil propensities to contend with and individual, separate desires and wills and interests to fulfill. He is now above all such thoughts and feelings, and therefore above all good and evil. He is the absolute good—if that conveys any meaning.[73]

He is all-loving, despising none. He cannot help it, because all are parts of himself in conscious feeling and experience—all things and beings are only himself in diverse forms; as Brahman, "all-knowing and all things he becomes; he sees himself in all

---

[73] This is the real meaning and explanation of certain passages which have been erroneously interpreted as sanctioning unbridled license on the part of Freed Man. On the transcending of ethical distinctions see Brih. Up. 4.3.22; Chāndogya Up. 4.14.3; Mundaka Up. 3.1.3; Prashna Up. 5.5. The full significance of such passages will be understood by comparison with the saying of St. Augustine,

and all in himself."

He is fearless. Whom can he fear? All are only aspects of himself. What can he fear? He is not the body, which, as body, he now feels to be no more himself than the clothes he may be wearing, and he has no personal and separate interests, no individual possessions, power, name, fame, and reputation; he can therefore have no fear of injury to any of them by anyone. He is in conscious experience Brahman, the heart and soul and spirit, the inmost Self of every thing and being. He is the inmost Self even of the Angels (Devas), who are now subject to his will and he to the will of none. He is therefore utterly fearless.

He is a conquering hero, having triumphed over all sorrow and suffering and all privations that limited life is heir to. He has the power to prevent any suffering coming to him. But he does not run away from an occasion or a circumstance that may be the cause of suffering, may affect or injure his body and whatever may pertain to it. He has no desire to run away from these; for he knows that such occasions for injury or destruction to his body can arise only in payment of the last remnants of his moral and spiritual obligations (*karma*) incurred in the past on account of his now transcended individuality.[74]

"Love God and do what you will."

[74] Such remnants of moral and spiritual debts are technically called Prārabdha Karma, Karma that has already begun its operation, and is only one of three classes into which Karma was analyzed in later times, but, no doubt, in accordance with principles underlying the idea of Karma as treated in the Vedic texts. The three classes of Karma are:

1. The Karma which is being produced by thought or action at any particular time and will subsequently come to fruition (*kriyamāna*). Of this newly created Karma only a small portion can find its ultimation in that same lifetime; the major portion remains latent as a cause of events and character in a subsequent life.

2. The Karma which, not having found an opportunity of bringing about the appropriate results during the incarnation in which it was produced, has gone on accumulating from ages past and is

Thus lives the man who has realized himself fully and experienced his ultimate Self as one with the Self of all the Universe. Pure and soft as a lily, and yet strong and fearless, loving and joyous, he continues his life on earth, singing, as it were, the song of triumph and of oneness with all things and beings.[75]

But joyous and happy as they are and free from every obligation of life, these perfected beings of

---

waiting for a suitable opportunity to show itself in results (*samcita*).

3. The Karma selected out of this accumulated heap in such a manner that the selected portions can produce results without being mutually nullifying (*prārabdha*).

It is this Prārabdha Karma which determines the present incarnation of a soul with all its possibilities, both subjectively in regard to a man's character and capacities and objectively in regard to situation and environment. Prārabdha Karma has to be self-consistent, as otherwise it cannot work. For instance, it cannot be such that it will make a man both blind and full-visioned from birth or both poor and wealthy throughout life.

Prārabdha Karma is, moreover, obligation which one must face and endure or enjoy as the case may be. It is not possible to escape it, and often it is not morally right to attempt to shirk it. It is not right to shirk it because by so doing a person strengthens the feeling of separateness, which, in other words, is selfishness and leads him away from the ultimate goal of life, namely the realization of oneness. It will be observed that one never shirks duty except for selfish reasons—fear, idleness, and the like. Hence a Yogin does not run away from Prārabdha Karma, that is, duties and obligations of life, even when he can do so, but performs them to the uttermost, even unto death. While Prārabdha must be faced, the accumulated Karma, which is held together by a man's unconscious ego, is destroyed as soon as this ego is destroyed, on the realization of oneness, and accumulated Karma, which readily constituted his individuality, is seen in positive experience as something other than his real Self, now realized as one with the Self of all.

[75] What the measure of the joy and love (*ānanda*) of the Freed Man may be has been described in two striking passages in the Upanishads. The most perfect and ideal state of bliss for a human being, as human, is taken as the unit. We are then told how the bliss of the next stage of spiritual advancement or next higher state of superhuman existence is a hundred times the unit of the most perfect human bliss; and how the bliss of the third stage is a hundred times that of the second, and so on; till we come to a measure of bliss which, as expressed in an arithmetical figure, is really inconceivable. And this inconceivably and immeasurably great bliss is finally held up as the bliss of Brahman and of the Freed Man who has realized oneness with Brahman. See Brih. Up. 4.3.33; Taittirīya Up. 2.8.

transcendent experience are never idle. On the contrary, they—the "Great Ones (mahāntas), full of Peace, saintly—live and work, without noise, naturally, like the season of Spring that, unobserved, makes all of Nature smile with joy. They have themselves crossed over to the other side of the fearful ocean of repeated births and deaths and help others to cross it without seeking a reward."[76]

When such a great soul of Divine Freedom cannot, or is not required to, be of service in any specific manner, it is held that he is even then of the greatest service to mankind by his very presence with us.

Then, when all duties are done and all obligations of the past are paid back and the time comes for him to discard the mortal coil, as they say, he often does so by an act of the will.[77] And, the body discarded, he is pure unblemished Brahman, one with Him and yet somehow, as it were, a different center whence may well up a new universe of love and joy: he is now a new singer of a fresh universal song.

In Christian phraseology he has resurrected himself and risen from the rock-bound tomb of matter and materiality, from all Negation; neither can he "die any more," not being compelled to be born any more. He has become not only "equal unto the angels," but greater than they—indeed, their inmost and controlling self.[78]

He has become, as it were, a new creator, as he has reached everywhere, pure and shining, bodiless, with-

---

[76] Cf. Viveka-cūdāmani.

[77] With regard to death by an act of the will, see page 49 and note 36.

[78] Cf. Luke 20.36. It is noteworthy that the more typical way of expressing the idea of reincarnation in the older texts is not "rebirth" but "redeath" (punarmrityu). And the perfected man "overcomes repeated death" (apa punarmrityum jayati, Brih. Up. 1.2.7). In view of this fact the expression used in Luke 20.36, "neither can they die any more," is very striking indeed.

out disease, one with Awareness that needs no instrument of bodily nerves, untouched by evil. For all eternity, he has now become the dispenser of the joys, yea, even of the sorrows, of life to beings as yet away from the divine home, dispensing these according to their various deserts, according as is right and just.[79]

Such is the end, such the consummation of life, of Man—in the Vedic view.

---

[79] Cf. Prashna Up. 4.10: *sa sarvajñah, sarvo bhavati,* and many other passages in praise of the finally freed man.

Cf. also Īshā Upanishad 8, which, it may be noted, refers to the man who has the oneness with all mentioned in the two immediately preceding Mantras.

It may be noted here that the Christian doctrine of Christ "judging the quick and the dead" seems hardly different from the Vedic idea of the Freed Man who has been dispensing things according to their rightness (*yāthātathyato 'rthān vyadadhac chāshvatībhyah samābhyah,* Īshā Up. 8).

EPILOGUE

The following benediction in the words of the great Hindu poet and dramatist Kālidāsa[80] forms a beautifully conceived epitome—and may thus be regarded as a fitting conclusion—of the sublime outlook on life that is set forth in the foregoing pages:

> *Vedānteshu yam ahur Eka-Purusham vyāpya*
> *sthitam rodasī yasminn Ishvara-ity ananya-*
> *vishayah s h a b d o yathārthāksharah antar*
> *yash ca mumukshubhir niyamita-prānādibhir*
> *mrigyate sa sthānuh sthira-bhakti-yoga-sulabho*
> *nihshreyasāyāstu vah.*

This may be interpretatively rendered into English as follows:

> May He whom in the "Veda-Ends"[81] they call the one, the only true Person, established firm, pervading the "ever-roaring twins"[82] [of Life's straight and curving lines[83] that are the warp and woof of heaven and earth and all];
>
> In whom the sonance Lord, unmeaning elsewhere, doth find its true significance;
>
> Who is sought within their inmost soul, by those desiring Freedom, with all movings of life, thought, and passions hushed and controlled;

---

[80] Vikramorvashīyam 1.1.
[81] That is, in the Upanishads.
[82] This word, *rodasī*, from *rud*, "to roar, cry," is of the same meaning as the word *krandasī* occurring in RV. 2.12.8; 6.25.4; 10.121.6.
[83] See above, pages 44-45.

Who yet is easy to attain by the art of unshaking,
all-forgetting love[84]—may He, the unmoving Pillar of all that moves and lives, be unto your
attaining That which is the Unsurpassable Good,
the Supreme Worth.[85]

---

[84] The term *bhakti* is defined as *parānuraktir Īshvare,* "all-surpass-
ing, supreme love for the Lord."

[85] Absolute Freedom, the state of abiding Being, unconditioned
Awareness, and unmixed Joy and Love.

SUPPLEMENTARY NOTES

A. *On Vivarta, the Athanasian Creed, and the Christian View of Immanence*

The writer of the foregoing pages has been told by several persons that the idea that the one ultimate Divine Being apparently divides himself and appears in countless forms as the universe, yet without undergoing in himself any change whatsoever (page 22 above), is to them strange and difficult of comprehension. This conception of the universal process, technically called *vivarta*, is, however, not entirely foreign to Christianity.

The Athanasian Creed, when it speaks of the one God becoming three persons "without dividing the substances," is undoubtedly expressing a similar idea, except that the conception of God entertained by the average Christian of ancient and modern times is that of an extracosmic entity and quite "naïve and anthropomorphic." This was the case, according to Professor McGiffert, even with Jesus (*The God of the Early Christians*, New York, 1924, page 4). It is, however, a view which the present writer does not believe to be correct, even though the synoptic Gospels—on which Professor McGiffert relies for his statement, and which are now recognized to be later than the letters of Paul and written by Jews who were naturally predisposed to see their own ancestral conceptions in the teachings of Jesus—may have represented Jesus as holding such an idea. On the contrary, the conception of the Deity held by Jesus was really that of a Being who is certainly immanent in every living soul, in every thing and being, so that Jesus could proclaim: "Behold, the kingdom of God is within you" (Luke 17.21) , putting into the phrase "kingdom of God" a new meaning totally at variance with any conception the Hebrews might have had about their own theocratic "kingdom." That he also believed in the transcendent aspect of the Deity is obvious from the fact that the average Christian, basing his belief on the teachings of Jesus, regards his God as something away from this world, somewhere in the upper heavens, where, he further believes, Jesus himself went up in his physical body when he "rose from the dead," as the saying is. That this is only a naïve, popular way of regarding the idea of transcendence can hardly be doubted.

In any case, the Vedic doctrine of *vivarta* and immanence should not be considered strange now, in view of the epoch-making statement, in the encyclical accompanying the resolution of the Lambeth Conference of 1930, saying: "Scientific thinking and discovery seems to be giving us back the sense of reverence and awe before the Creator, *Who is not only the cause and ground of the universe, but is always everywhere and active within it.*" (The italics are the present writer's.)

This is exactly the view which the Vedic Indians and those incorporated in their communities have held from time immemorial. Only it should be added that, in the Vedic view, the Divine Being is not only immanent in the universe as the only ground, the only substance, and the ceaseless controller of all that is, there being no other substance, controller, or abiding reality whatsoever, but he is also, at the same time and forever, a transcendent Being, beyond and above all relation to the universe: he is, in other words, at once both the Transcendent and the Immanent Deity, "without dividing the substance."

B. *On the Term "Dullness"*

Professor E. Washburn Hopkins, who has laid the writer under a deep debt of obligation by his careful and sympathetic consideration of the foregoing pages, has raised only one serious objection, as follows:

"I should like to suggest that *āvarana* (on page 80) is a *māyāshakti* of an active nature just like *vikshepa* in being an activity (antithetic to *vikshepa*), and as you render *vikshepa* quite rightly by 'distraction,' so *āvarana* is not the passive negative 'dullness' itself, but the cause of the dullness, and it is so because it is literally the 'closure' or 'immurement,' that is, an active power, suppressing and so making the mind dull, rather than the dullness itself; 'shutting up' or 'bolting in' the mind (*āvarana* actually means a 'bolt' as well as the more common activity of 'enclosing'). I do not know whether this will appeal to you, but that is the way it seems to me, especially as *āvarana* and *vikshepa* are defined as *shaktidvayam* (two antithetic powers) and dullness results from *āvarana,* just as a lack of concentration does from *vikshepa*."

The writer fully agrees with Professor Hopkins and accepts this kindly criticism. He believed, however, that from what was said about the true nature of the universal process as being the manifestation of a living, conscious, and active Energy (*shakti*), starting with the tremendous act of negating and suppressing the abiding Being himself—an act which produces the first notion of Universal Nothingness—it would be understood by readers that even "dullness," like sleep, though apparently passive, was really due to the operation of an active energy. The writer is, however, grateful to Professor Hopkins for drawing attention to what evidently might easily be misunderstood and for giving him this opportunity of clearing the matter up.

INDEX

A

Absorption, 25, 72
Agni, 58, 59, 61
Aham Kara, 30, 34, 37, 51, 70
Air, 29, 57, 61
Ākāsha, 28-30, 49, 51-58, 61
Ānanda, 18, 24, 35, 71
Anna, 27, 71
Anu, 17, 59, 68
Ap, 59, 61
Asat, 31, 37, 41, 50-51, 71
Atman, 16-19, 26-27, 36-42, 48,
    51, 54-55, 61-62, 64, 67, 69,
    71-72, 74, 79, 85, 87
Avidyā, 37, 50, 51, 89
Awareness, 18, 19, 35

B

Being, 16, 18-19, 22, 35-36,
    67-68
Bhūta, 27, 37, 49-50, 61
Bhūta-Mātrā, 37, 42, 49, 56-60
Brahman, 20, 24-26, 39, 42, 48,
    67, 69-70, 72, 77, 79, 82,
    87-90, 92
Brāhmanas, 13
Browning, Robert, 79
Buddha, 37-38, 76, 86
Buddhi, 34

C

Causal Body, 36
Chit, 18
Christ Principle, 36, 39
Concentration, 80-81
Concrete Mentality, 30-33, 36,
    44-45, 48, 50-51
Continuity, 15, 47
Continuum, 27-29

D

Devas, 38, 64, 68, 76, 82, 89, 90
Dharma, 77
Dishah, 54-55

E

Earth, 29, 60-61, 69
Ego, 30, 33-34, 37, 40, 42-43,
    47, 51
Elements, 29, 61
Entities, 41
Eshanā, 45, 48
Ether, 28
Evolution, 70

F

Fire, 29, 56, 58-59, 61

The Theosophical Publishing House is the exclusive distributor in North and South America of books published by the Adyar Library and Research Centre, Madras, India. Send for our free catalog of books on the following subjects:

Agama — Astrology — Buddhism
Indian Ethics, Law, Political Science
Indian Grammar and Linguistics — The Gita
Indian Civilization and Culture — Lexicography
The Philosophy of Mimamsa — Indian Music and Dance
The Nyaya Philosophy — Prakrit Literature
Indian Poetics and Dramaturgy — The Upanishads
The Vedas — Vedanta — Yoga

All available from:
The Theosophical Publishing House
306 West Geneva Road
Wheaton, Illinois 60187